Return of the Bones

MAGIC PROSE Publisher

ISBN: 1-4751-8742-4
ISBN-13: 9781475187427
Library of Congress Control Number: 2012906916
CreateSpace, North Charleston SC

Return of the Bones

Belinda Vasquez Garcia

With special thanks to Bobby for steering me in the right direction.

Dedication

With loving memory, Return of the Bones is dedicated to the ghosts of Pecos.

Though they be extinct, they are cloud people who move gently over the ruins of Pecos Pueblo.

Though they have died out, they are not forgotten.

Their spirit lives on in the Jemez people and all indigenous peoples of earth.

From their toil, a civilization was built.

From their imagination, a legend was born.

From their bones, medical science expanded.

May their fire of Montezuma burn brightly.

May their feathered serpent awaken.

And may they cross over to the other side where Pautiwa, Chief of Kachina Village, awaits.

Table of Contents

Other books by Belinda Vasquez Garcia

Short nonfiction in eBooks

The Bigamist, A Memoir of My Father

The Womanizer, Another Memoir of My Father

Novels in both paperback and eBooks

I Will Always Love You

The Witch Narratives Reincarnation (Land of Enchantment 1)

Ghosts of the Black Rose (Land of Enchantment 2)

http://belindavasquezgarcia.com/

AUTHOR'S NOTE

Return of the Bones is a novel based on a true story few are familiar with in Native American history. A glossary has been included at the end of the book. Please refer to the Table of Contents for the page number.

Included at the end of the story is a section entitled *Interactive Links* with a list of hyperlinks, related to the book, found at http://magicprose.com.

There is, also, a *Reading Guide* with suggested discussion questions for book clubs and reading groups at http://magicprose.com/guide.

Although the bones be hundreds of years old, they are still family. For blood flows from generation to generation and thus, the family line lives on.

I

After ninety-eight years of hard living, the only mystery Grandfather could not crack was how to die in peace and leave this world in a gentler way than he endured it. He harbored many secrets, including his true heritage: he was not a Jemez Indian. He and his thirty-five-year-old granddaughter, Hollow-Woman, were the last of their kind, survivors of the ghost pueblo of Pecos. The lines on his face traced a family tree. Often, he led her on a funeral dance across the branches by pointing out which wrinkle on his face sprouted after a relative's death. He waltzed across creases of his great-grandparents, grandparents, mother, father, stepmothers, brothers, sisters, cousins, uncles, aunts, in-laws, children, relatives she never knew. His lineage criss-crossed his features like a New Mexico roadmap. He masked his soul's potholes with poetry he recited in their native tongue Towa.

"Granddaughter, you are but a splinter from the pine trees of Pecos. I dreamed that from a splinter a tree would blossom with many branches, but I quake in my moccasins that the Pecos people will die with you."

"Blah-blah-blah-blah-blah. You jabber like a broken record, old man; family, ghosts and a fallen pueblo relic." Hollow-Woman blew on her manicure and two fang marks on her forehead opened and closed. He could see right through her snake scars and believed he had the means to save her. Lord knows he tried ever since saddled with her at four days old. Her parents died and abandoned her to the care of this imposing Shaman who never taught her how to be kind.

"Geronimo!" blared from the speaker and she sighed with relief that he forgot about barren women and extinction.

He peered with bloodshot eyes at the twenty-six inch screen that broadcast a tad fuzzy due to rabbit ears and poor reception at Jemez, isolated like most pueblos.

A woman reporter, dressed in navy blue suit and stiff collar, wiggled about in snow. "A letter written in 1918 has been discovered in the Sterling Memorial Library archive that refers to Yale University students stealing Geronimo's bones. The Apache warrior's bones vanished in 1918 from his grave at Fort Sill, Oklahoma and bragging rights have circulated at Yale for decades that his bones were at the elite Skull and Bones Society's headquarters. It is said that Geronimo's skull is displayed in a glass case and used to initiate new members into the secretive order. One of the thieves is purported to be George Prescott Bush, the deceased father of George H. W. Bush, former President of the United States. The letter, written from one Bonesman to another Bonesman, reveals details of the 1918 theft and may be proof that the rumor is true, as the Apaches have claimed for years—former students stole Geronimo's bones as a Yale prank."

He seemed bewildered at the woman's report. Hollow-Woman acted as his English interpreter since seven years of age, after returning for the summer from St. Mary's Boarding School for Indians. Her head had reached his waist and English as choppy as a category-five hurricane blew from her lips. She had since grown enough to look down at him and graduated to a category-one. She sat him down, like a child, and explained in Towa the deer meat and legumes of the news.

He turned white as a sheep. "The white man is not content with having chased us to the ends of the earth in life. They must come after us in death. Even our president."

"These are not the old days, Governor. In this case, justice will prevail. Geronimo's family can file with NAGPRA to get his bones back," she said.

"What is NAGPRA?"

"NAGPRA stands for Native American Graves Protection and Repatriation Act. I think Congress passed the bill in 1990. Using that law, Geronimo's family has the right to get his bones back."

"Geronimo's family and I have a bone to pick with rich white men, or in my case, many bones. So much lost time, nine years. I am a man teetering on death's crevice, and I must have a word with the ghosts of Pecos." He raised his eyes to the ceiling and ripped his shirt in two. He chanted the lyrics from a funeral song and wailed.

"Calm down, Governor."

He smiled in his mysterious way, his eyes appearing as two slits, carved into cracked mud.

"Crazy old Shaman," she said under her breath.

He leaned against their other heirloom, a royal ceremonial silver staff King Philip III of Spain presented to their clan in 1620. At that time, Pecos Pueblo was the biggest town in what is now the United States. The silver was so tarnished the staff was black, though she could see the reflection of her eye where he had rubbed his thumb across the staff for nearly a century. He had always been governor of the Ghost Pueblo of Pecos, their glory days long behind them. He claimed their conquerors did not vanquish them to the point of extinction, but a dying fire cursed them and their feathered serpent hid from them.

Other than the times he drank or smoked handmade cigarettes, his mouth remained closed. Usually he grunted. Normally his grunt revealed whether he hungered, boiled over, froze or whatever, but a sorry grunt never came from him. He now gave a pathetic grunt mixed with a whine. He wobbled away from the television on legs bowed from nearly a century spent riding horses. His petrified toe peeked through his canvas high-top tennis shoes, the modern Indian moccasin, only he was trapped in a time warp of the glory days of the pueblos, before the invaders came. He pounded the royal staff against the cracked tile as if he was somebody, king of the Pecos Pueblo ruins. His long-sleeved shirt hung half-way out of his pants, the khaki dangling to his knees because he shrunk half an inch every year since he turned ninety. Oil and grass stains dotted his clothes. A gallon of bleach would not make his grey t-shirt white again.

"Crazy as a loon," she grumbled. They struggled on washing day. He claimed his magic's perspiration seeped into the threads of his clothes and detergent weakened his wizardry. It seemed they always locked horns. Ever since she was a little girl, his sorcery scared the hell out of her. His powers could do with a bit of dilution and he could do with a bath.

She wrinkled her nose at his greasy braids that swung around the wall, tucked her bare feet under her legs and went back to watching the news. The report switched to the coming of the Millennium in nine months, a panic that claimed the world was due to end because all the computers would come crashing down due to the birth of the Y2K bug.

He wasted no time returning to the living room and blocking her view of the television with his five-foot three-inch frame. He waved like a swaying tree with his urine-stained mattress slumped across his spine.

She rose to help him but the mattress slid off his back.

He swung his neck and took a swig from a bottle of wine encased in a paper sack; as if he could fool her into thinking he drank Kool-Aid. He smacked his lips and shoved the cork back on. He nudged her shoulder.

"Drive me to Pecos. Bring my mattress; I would like to ride in comfort on my own bed for my last journey home."

"You can't call Pecos home. The ancestors deserted the pueblo a century and a half ago. Even you can't claim to be that ancient, Governor."

He filled her childhood with horror when he first took her to the godforsaken family pueblo and spoke about the Spanish Inquisition, church torchings, beheadings, blood spilling, ghosts, witches, and poisonings. She screamed whenever he wanted to go to the haunted Pecos ruins. Last time he dragged her to Pecos she was twelve and swore then never to go back but now, he pleaded with his eyes and he was so damned old. So, she heaved his mattress and hauled the saggy, smelly thing behind her, stopping now and then to smack at the fleas. She zigzagged to her pickup-truck, pulling his mattress through the mud holes, just to be ornery.

Huffing and puffing, she lifted his mattress and shoved it into the bed of her pickup. Her head spun from the stench of wine wafting from the faded grey and white stripes. Her truck lived up to a junk man's dream with cigarette butts, cans, bottles, rags, and other sundries scattered about. Like him, she never threw anything away, a habit nourished by a childhood of poverty.

She jerked open the passenger door, but he lifted a leg over the back and plopped down on his mattress. He stared at the sky with glazed eyes. His head appeared like a shriveled cranberry. With a shaky hand he clutched a blanket to his chin, spittle dribbling down his neck.

He had few teeth to speak of and his skinny body did not even dent his mattress. He just lay there with his arms and legs spread wide, croaking like a frog.

"But, Governor, you'll catch a chill. Why don't we wait until Steve's day off so we can travel in his car?"

"Death stalks me like a sunset shadow but I shall outfox the pale horse and with bridle and lasso, ride fifteen minutes more after the sun skis down the Sangre de Cristo Mountains. Remember, Granddaughter, build my coffin from pine trees of the Sangre de Cristos."

"Don't speak of dying," she whispered.

"Do not weep like a willow in the snow. Reunion with the snake clan is like a dance at winter solstice. Like the prodigal son in the Bible, family will join hands and dance around me to Masawkatsina's drums and the Keeper of the Dead will welcome me with open arms."

"Stop talking nonsense and ride in the front with me. It's mid-February. You'll catch pneumonia."

"I long for the wind blowing on my face. I wish to breathe crisp air into my lungs. I will be confined in a box soon enough, and the elements will not kill me, but my body's weakness will be the death of me. Your new truck must be good for something, to carry my coffin."

"Eight years ago a new used truck, now my truck free and clear," she said, lifting her chin proudly but regretting choosing a black pickup since he equated her truck to a hearse.

He banged the damn staff against metal; she jumped.

"Bring my knapsack, it has my ceremonial pipe," he ordered.

With black hair swinging around her waist, she marched into her mud house made of adobe blocks that resembled all the other houses at the Jemez Pueblo, making it appear like a village from the Stone Age.

She stuck her tongue out at the mirror, wishing she did not always give into him, especially when his health was at stake. She lacked the courage of a Pecos warrior though her Native American ancestry shone from her naturally tanned skin and high cheekbones.

She stomped back carrying his knapsack, and threw it on the front seat.

"Drive," he barked and whopped that frickin' staff as if heir to a kingdom and not a curse.

"Quit having a tantrum," she said, fitting a pair of fluffy earmuffs on his ears. She wrapped his neck with a muffler, pulling the wool to just below his nose. She shoved his hat on his head, wrapped him in a blanket, and tucked his legs and hips into a sleeping bag. She yanked up the zipper so the bag wouldn't fly off him.

The governor of Pecos laid wrapped like a papoose, a forgotten mummy, the royal ceremonial staff beside him. He had spoken of his impending death. He was old and the bright sun was deceiving; over to the east towards Pecos grey clouds gathered.

"What if it rains?" she said.

"It will not rain. I have not called forth any storms today."

"Right, Weatherman."

He squeezed his eyes shut and his lower lip trembled. The tip of his nose was wet.

"I'll take you home to Pecos, Governor, if this is your wish," she said and sighed, stroking his withered cheek. Thank goodness his skin wasn't hot.

He jerked his head away from her fingers.

She climbed on the driver's seat and slammed the door, cussing under her breath. Stubborn old man refused to ride up front with her. She hated the Pecos ruins, the most depressing place ever. Years had passed...

She cranked up the engine to drive from the Jemez Pueblo, the eighty miles to the Pecos Pueblo. The tires wobbled along the unpaved sections of Blue Bird Mesa. She peeked at the rear view mirror and cocked her ear for any groans coming from the back. The gas pedal vibrated beneath her foot, whether to speed up her pickup towards the paved New Mexico Highway Four or slow the truck down—prolong his agony or worsen his pain while they sped along the bumps. His urgency when he mentioned Pecos made her shove her foot harder on the pedal.

She merged onto I-25, headed north towards Santa Fe, and passed the capital. The truck climbed towards the Sangre de Cristo Mountains. A bit of snow covered the pine trees and hopefully, the truck bed and sleeping bag would keep the cool air from penetrating his bones. She should have covered his entire face with the blanket but feared smothering him.

"We're here, Governor."

She jammed her foot on the brakes and climbed out of the truck. She stood on tiptoes to see if he survived the journey.

Almost a century nibbled away at his muscles, yet he found the strength to reach his shriveled fingers over the side and sit while she unhooked the tailgate. He unzipped the sleeping bag and with her help climbed down. He covered his shoulders with the blanket.

"You took off your earmuffs," she said.

"Bah. Why would I want to silence my ears?"

"What happened to the new hat I bought you?"

"The wind gave the hat wings," he said, thrusting his chin out.

"You flung your hat away on purpose."

"My old hat suits me like bottle rockets." He yanked a blackish round hat from around his back. "The sweat of my magic fills this hat. It serves me in spring when Brother Rain soaks my beaten path; in summer when Father Sun sweats my ivory tower; in fall when Brother Wind blows me contrary; and in winter when Brother Snow powders my lashes like a vintage whore."

She shoved the brim lower on his head and rolled her eyes at his hat that did not appear enchanted because Father Time smashed and crushed the feather. He wore this hat for more than five decades, with his head growing bigger each time he rose in pueblo status, so the hat now barely reached his forehead.

"You are vintage wine turned to vinegar so we better wrap you good," she said, twisting the blanket tighter around his shoulders and sniffing the wool. She knitted this blanket when a teenager with five thumbs and the patches as rough as the road between them yet, the old man cared for it all these years, and prized her gift as a most cherished possession. He never once told her he loved her. Perhaps his heart broke into so many pieces; maybe he feared getting too close in case she died before him like the rest of his family. She most resented him for the deepest dents on his cheeks that he never dragged her fingers across. These lines cast shadows of her parents' lives. Even a wrench wouldn't pry him open so she knew little about her mother and father.

At five foot six, she was tall for a Native American woman and towered over him. She supported his left arm, resisting the urge to stretch her long legs while they walked.

Dust swirled like brown ghosts around her ankles, causing her to shiver. Wind howling through the rubble chilled her to the bone. She cursed his senility and kicked the red dirt, this precious dirt he loved so much, this place filled with broken dreams. Ever since she was a small child, he drilled into her the story of how God created man in Shipapu. Man made his way up from Shipapu to the Fourth Womb of Existence, the red earth of Pecos, where Father Sun and Mother Moon smiled upon their children for the very first time. This Garden of Eden had always disappointed her, which, besides the ruins, consisted of cholla cactus, pinion trees and juniper. There was beauty only in yellow flowers on the chamisa bushes.

What had not eroded of her inheritance included about twenty ceremonial kivas, holes deep in the earth big enough to hold a couple dozen people? No one but him could believe the spirits of the gods once dwelled below. Pecos Pueblo appeared deserted by not only the gods of the Indian but also the God of their Spanish conquerors. The jagged adobe rust-red remnants of the Spanish mission still dominated, but what remained of the Spanish Catholic Church were merely ragged pieces of adobe wall yet...yet if she closed her eyes, she heard church bells ringing. She could see Franciscan friars clothed in monks' robes, rosary beads clanking against their knees, hoods bowed and chanting novenas as they entered the church. This was no mere church but the first cathedral in New Mexico with three spiraling towers on each side and hollow walls so thick, the Franciscans held services in not just the main church interior but between the walls where the congregation spilled over. Now, only ghosts worshipped at this site and the towers were...well she plopped down on one of the towers and crossed her knees. She clasped her gloved hands and tongue-in-cheek, blinked her eyes at him.

"Let's go. I've seen enough, Governor," she said.

He stared at her as if hypnotized; his eyes bugged out of his head. He clawed at her neck and whimpered. Perhaps he needed to piss but then a howl rose from so deep within his being; it seemed his very soul cried out. He dug his fingernails into her shoulders and shook her. "We must bring home the ones stolen from their graves," he said.

"There aren't any marked graves here."

"Bah. Don't treat me like a child, Girl," he said, slapping her hand away.

"You are wrong, Woman," he roared and pounded the earth with his staff. "There are graves buried deep below this earth. Six centuries of death and of living, joys and sorrows are sifted into these ashes. Strong winds may have mixed the dirt of other pueblos with ours, but deep beneath this layer of dust our family is buried. Like dew on my heart, you have bellyached that your friends had cousins, aunts and uncles, brothers and sisters, and you had no one but a tired, old man. Here is your family, in the red earth of Pecos." He scooped a handful of dirt, opened her hand and spilled the dirt into her palm. He closed her fist and squeezed.

"Your family lived on this red earth since the year 1300. Before that time we were known as the Forked Lightning people who climbed from the arroyo to this ridge and built an impenetrable fortress. Our people were born here; they married here; they made love here; they died here. You say this is a ghost pueblo and you are right. Pecos chimes a death knell since the thief stole the others and took them far away from the land that nourished them. Tears flow from the skies for thousands ripped from the earth. Can you not feel the earth shudder like a body racked with grief? Can you not see how tears, of those left behind, moisten the earth because they mourn the missing? Can you not hear the wind sigh with longing?"

He shoved the royal ceremonial staff into her hands and squeezed her fingers around it. "Feel your people's pride and imagine this staff must have been something to look at in those days when the Pecos governor pounded it against the rich dirt, and his people surveyed their bounty. Now, the staff is dull and can you not see their disenchantment with their invaders?"

He pushed the staff to her ear. "Listen to your inheritance and the cries of your people."

He lifted the staff to her nose. "Inhale their blood."

He finished his speech and the wind blew a silence across the ruins. He communed with the wind and the earth so that his emotions swirled with the pueblo remains. He appeared made from Pecos dirt, his skin reddish-brown.

She pushed the staff back at him and he looked like he wanted to throttle her.

"As you know, pueblo is the Spanish word for people. My Pecos Pueblo, which you scorn, is proof of a forgotten people, save what I hold in my heart. Our people were the chosen ones. Each year more of Pecos vanishes until one day there will be nothing left. Look at rings that still show upon the earth from tipis set up for trade fairs over centuries of prosperity. Ah, my home is melting back into dirt from which it was made."

His eyes glowed with the delirium of peyote. He was just coming down from a high.

"I don't believe you about the stolen corpses; how could you possibly know?"

"I know," he said, thumping his chest with his fist.

"But Pecos was a ghost pueblo sixty-two years before your birth," she said.

"I was thirteen winters old when I watched thousands unearthed from the rich soil that nurtured them. I wondered if I knew any of the skeletons. My father? My grandparents? My great-grandparents? Mother? Brothers and sisters? We no longer lived at Pecos then, but always we returned to be buried where our roots were planted. Like a coward, I hid behind a tree and watched the grave robbers. I told myself as the last of our people, I had a duty to survive. I stood over there." He teetered on tobacco-stained khakis and pointed with a shaky finger to a ridge lined with trees. One tree appeared to wilt compared to others. He squeezed his eyes shut and spasms racked his body.

Surely his tears will petrify into more wrinkles.

"With my death you are the last of the Pecos. A heavy burden falls upon your shoulders. Promise me, you will bring the bones home."

He jabbed an imploring finger at her and the scar on her forehead throbbed. At the age of seven, a rattlesnake slithered across her bed, locked eyes with her, jerked its head back, opened its fangs, and marked her right above her nose. She always rubbed her scar when nervous and jumpy, and Grandfather hissed at her so that poison snaked through her veins. She dug her fingernails into her palms; she could strike out just as hurtful.

"I feel nothing for old bones and a pueblo abandoned a century and a half ago. What do I care for roots, when I may be the last branch to fall? Our tree's dry, Governor. Live with it," she drawled.

He thumped his heart with his fist and accused her of being hollow. He preached as unforgiving as the rain, snow and wind that ravaged the family pueblo for one hundred and sixty-one years. Even her husband Steve could not fill the cracks in her heart. She let Grandfather down so many times and put more wrinkles on his face. All her life he was old, but her earliest memory of him was with grey hair. His head whitened because of her. Now she could not promise to look for some ancient skeletons he claimed stolen from Pecos. He sent goose bumps across her spine when he spoke about missing bones.

"I see I have not touched you, Granddaughter, by bringing you to Pecos. I raised you since four days old, but failed to teach you about your ancestors. You were born with a spirit as wild as the Río Grande rapids, and I am not a patient man. In vain, I tried to make you appreciate the bond of one's blood. How do I get through to you that Pecos is our home?"

He clenched her hand and shocked her with his strength but then he always blew in like a force of nature; even old as he was, his eyes shone with invincibility.

"Look with your heart, not your eyes, and see that our pueblo's spirit yet lives. Even Moctezuma could not crush the heart of a people," he said.

"He answered to Montezuma," she said, yanking at her wrist but he stubbornly held on, like all the other Pueblo Indians who insisted the legend was true.

He could tell by her eyes that she really did not believe and he flung her wrist from him.

"Look around you and see the proof of Moctezuma's curse," he said, sweeping his hand across the earth.

"How many times must I tell you that Moctezuma was a witch born at the ancient Pose Uingge Pueblo in New Mexico? After he grew up, he traveled to the Pecos Pueblo where he changed his name to Montezuma and ruled. Under Montezuma, Pecos flourished and became overpopulated so he decided to form other New Mexico pueblos with the surplus. He then flew on an eagle south and founded more pueblos in New Mexico and then the great Mexico City. Before he left Pecos, he lit a fire at the Altar of the Sun. He demanded twelve virgins tend the fire, so that Pecos would prosper until his return. The people promised him they would keep the fire lit and wait for him to come back to them."

"Yes and Montezuma never returned to Pecos because the virgins who tended the fire fell asleep one balmy night and let the fire die out. The pueblo then burned less brightly, weakening with each passing year, until the day the flame was snuffed out and just ashes remained of Pecos. Blah-blah-blah," she said, rolling her eyes.

"Look around you at the wreckage and see this is no legend but truth."

Her shoulders sagged and the wind pushed against her. How ironic the bloody earth of Pecos appeared so healthy and able to nurture life while she appeared so pale and lifeless. It seemed as if the people's blood flowed in the earth, turning the dirt a rich red in color, while in her own veins weak blood circulated.

"Governor, if you're so concerned about my being the last then I should try harder to conceive instead of trying to find some old bones no one cares about except you," she said with a resentful voice. She turned her back to him and wiped her damp eyes. She squeezed her waist with her elbows and held back her memories but her losses seeped through her brain like a sponge soaked with afterbirth. Her first baby she miscarried in her first trimester. The second, a little girl, was miscarried in her second trimester. The third flowed watery blood that burst from her womb at two months. The fourth kicked vigorously at six months, then stilled a week later. The fifth baby, a girl, delivered stillborn. The sixth, a boy, breathed for four days, the same amount of time her father lived after her birth. The seventh, she never even told Steve about her pregnancy; ditto for her eighth attempt. The ninth was lost at seven weeks, a year ago. She and Steve were so heartbroken, they reconciled to a childless marriage, unknown to Grandfather. False hope would only shatter her fragilely mended heart, and she no longer had the strength or time to heal.

He surprised her when he let the blanket drop from his frail shoulders.

Her teeth clinked in her mouth like piano keys because the cowardly sun darted behind the mountains as if sensing the tension between them. She bent to pick up the blanket.

"Leave it," he said.

"Old man, you're going to get sick from your passion for these missing bones. If the bones mean so much to you, why didn't you find them?"

"I could never make my way in the white man's world."

"But your powers...surely..."

"If I, born in 1901, am so out of place in the white man's world then our bones, some centuries old, are even more lost. The people do not answer when I cry out to them. Our family circle is broken. You must find the bones so the people can be one again. If we must die out, then let us all join together."

"You want me to search for a bunch of skeletons, people dead and buried long before my birth, most before you were born? I have no idea where to even begin to look. Their bones may have scattered to the four corners of the world. Dust blows across the tracks of time and buries a cold trail. Which corner of the world shall I probe first, Governor?"

"You're a sly girl; find a way to bring the missing bones home with this NAPGRA."

"It's NAGPRA but I can't just up and quit my job to seek skeletons you claim stolen from Pecos."

"Perhaps this will help." He opened his burlap sack and handed her what looked like an old leather case.

She peeked inside the case filled with papers.

"I snuck down from my hiding place and took these papers that belonged to the grave robber. I cannot read but perhaps the thief left a clue to help you recover the bones."

"Why did you never speak about any of this before today?"

"I remained silent because I feared they would come for us, too. You would have listened with the wooden ears of the Kachina dolls you collect. My death has crawled slowly as a desert box turtle, but perhaps when my spirit leaves my body's shell, you will listen like Big Ears Kachina and want to learn more about your people."

"Don't speak as if you're already dead. These haunted ruins give me the jitters. I can feel the ghosts stirring and it makes me afraid."

"Never say the ghosts of Pecos frighten you. If after death, I drift in like the morning fog for a heart-to-heart in my sweat lodge, will you be scared?"

"No, I would not be panic-stricken at your ghost. You are my grandfather; why would you spook me?"

He must have known she lied because he looked even wilder. His face reddened and he clenched his fists.

He terrified her in life with his meanness. He never struck her but he had such a temper. He screamed at her when she first blundered across his rattlesnake den. He shook her until her teeth clattered. He barked at her to stay away from his beehives. Later, when older and wiser, she realized he only worried about her, but his presence commanded, and she cast a shadow under his feet. Well, she refused to make any effort for some old bones and if his ghost stalked her, then she would close her eyes to him. Pecos ravaged him all his life. This place of ruin would not wreck what little grasp of happiness she forged with Steve.

"I promise," she said in a flat voice merely to calm him so they could leave this land that chilled her blood.

She despised him for coercing her, and he knew it. He pleaded with his eyes for her to search for the bones, and cursed her with his lips. The threat in his voice had been real. He was most considerate friend to Masawkatsina so he possessed the means to haunt her in death, even more than he haunted her in life, if she did not find the bones.

Her only defense against his magic was a defiant look. Make him think he did not make her hands sweat. Look at the ground, so he could not see her eyes water. Take a deep breath so he did not hear her heart thumping. Yet, the ruins spun around her and made her dizzy. She stumbled, fell, and clawed the dirt at something flat and hard. What…the…yuck…a petrified toe attached to an ancient sandal.

"Don't touch the toe else the owner will follow in your footsteps," he said, jerking the sandal from her hand.

She scraped her fingernail across the ancient toe.

The now toeless sandal sailed through the air.

She ran after it, dropped to her knees and dug with her fingers, throwing dirt about, not caring if dust struck her face. But nothing, the sandal and toe vanished.

She wrapped her arms around her waist and rocked, cuffing her hands to her ears and screaming. Oh, God, a toeless Pecos ghost will haunt me. Her vertigo worsened so she stayed plopped down, crossed her arms and fooled him so he did not know she pressed against her chest. He must have tied her with a dozen invisible rubber bands.

His damn promise will be the death of me.

"I'm not Pecos; I'm Jemez," she said as if this sort-of fact would grant her absolution.

Acute pain crossed his face at her words.

She lowered her head and picked at a thread on her blouse, but her eyes stung like needle pricks.

Damn this guilt. Damn him.

She sprang up, dragged him to the truck, yanked open the front door and pushed him onto the front passenger seat.

His blanket caught on the door so the corner dragged against the ground.

She forced the key into the ignition and floored the gas pedal. The engine roared to life. The red earth of her ancestral home blew around the spinning tires, and she got the hell out of Pecos.

The old troublemaker bounced beside her on the springy seat, him too short to hit the ceiling with his head.

She turned on the radio to drown out any more lectures about family ties, bones, ghosts, or death.

Soon, his light snoring blew puffs of air between his lips. Spittle dribbled down his chin.

She rolled down the window and breathed the fresh air of life.

The heater blew on high for the old man whose chin rolled around his chest. He did not look so almighty when he slept nor so scary, so she shoved his hat low on his forehead so only his stubby eyelashes, crooked nose, and toothless mouth showed.

The truck descended away from the Sangre de Cristo Mountains. She merged onto I-25 and headed south towards Santa Fe.

The lights of the capital vanished from her rear view mirror miles back...When did his snoring stop?

She stole a glance at his still chest.

"Grandfather!"

She poked his arm.

His head fell against the windshield with a crack.

She jerked the steering wheel over to the shoulder and slammed on the brakes, bringing the tires to a screeching stop.

"Wake up," she begged, shaking him gently. "Please wake up."

The sun was just beginning to set. The spittle on his chin was frozen. He was already beginning to stiffen.

She threw items out of her purse until her fingers grasped her cell phone. Moonlight lit up the numbers 911. "He's dying," she cried out.

She cursed in Towa. The operator couldn't understand her choppy English accent and asked her not to grunt into the phone. The phone trembled as she slowly repeated, "He's dying. I think he's dead. He's not responding. Please hurry. What? No, I don't know exactly where I was when he died."

Three times she recited a description of her truck, her license plate number, more or less her location, then pressed the end button on her phone. The disconnection sounded like a heart monitor flat line.

She pounded her face against the steering wheel and moaned. She whizzed by about sixty miles of the eighty miles between Jemez Pueblo and Pecos Pueblo and could never backtrack to discover exactly where they were when he left her. She only knew that he left his heart at Pecos.

He claimed death shadowed him, yet he had no kind last words for her, no confession of eternal love, no begging for her forgiveness, no words of wisdom about life, only his damned promise to search for wretched bones.

With shaky hands, she reached for a paper sack and the shimmer of an unbroken seal of a whiskey bottle, but a pain so unbearable slammed against her chest that she grabbed for him instead.

"I'm sorry, so sorry," she said, rubbing her damp cheek against his soft white braids.

She wrapped her arms around his cold body and cradled his head to her breast, berating all the times she lashed out because she had no family except for him.

"Old man, old man, the only father and mother I have ever known," she said, rocking and howling like a wounded dog. She had not told him she loved him for such a long time, not since he screamed at her when she stood too close to his snake den at seven years of age.

I should have listened to your life. I could have watched for your death. I would have touched your heart, right there. She placed her hand over his chest and swore she felt the heartbeat of a Pecos warrior but it was probably the trembling of her hand.

"Even in death you smell like magic, Governor."

He proclaimed he would die how many minutes after sunset? She glanced at her watch and shook her wrist, as if she could turn back time.

"Oh, Grandfather, when did you die so silently beside me...and so alone?"

2

"He's not dead; he just had a slight heart attack," Steve said.

She cried in Steve's arms and peeked over his shoulder. Ah, look at the old man with no teeth and puckered lips; so skinny, mostly bones. His white hair swept his heart. He lay in a coma in an oxygen tent with tubes running into his chest, arms and stomach. He also suffered a slight stroke. The doctors marveled that at his age he held his own.

A priest arrived to administer the last rites, shoving her aside while he blessed his forehead.

"He has not worshipped Catholicism for years ever since he secretly joined the Native American Church," she said, pushing him back and quivering with anger that this man would just assume.

"Ah, so the poor soul is not Christian then. No wonder he worships in secret," the priest said.

"The American Indian Religious Freedom Act has allowed him for twenty-one years to practice his peyote religion openly. Our church believes in the Bible but we use peyote to commune with Jesus," Steve said.

She glared at the priest.

He spun on his heels and hastily left the room.

With shaky fingers, she covered Grandfather with another blanket. "He always complains of the cold and the swamp cooler. He's not going to die. That priest…" With long strides she hurried towards the exit and ran down the hall, holding a hand to her mouth. This Clorox-stinking hellhole must have a damned bathroom.

She barely made it to the toilet, folded over and emptied her stomach.

Steve waited for her at the bathroom exit. He wrapped his arm around her shoulder, led her to a chair, and grasped her hands in his.

"He knows you love him, Holly," he said.

She wiped her eyes, remembering Grandfather's wish for her to act strong and shuffled back to his room.

The case he gave her at Pecos had words engraved on the leather: *Dr. Alfred V. Kidder, Professor of Archaeology, Harvard University.* The case contained a black and white photo with the words, *Pecos Bones,* scrawled across the back along with the date *December 23, 1915.* The photo showed a slender, recent Ph.D. grad, an Indiana Jones wannabe, with burning ambition in his eyes that bespoke of a hunger for fame. He stroked his moustache with a delicate hand. The Pecos ruins drooped in the background of the photo, not as time-ravaged as present day. Dust caressed old-time trucks parked in the distance. Tents poked out from the earth like giant ant hills. He stood with hands on hips and puffed-out chest by a pile of bones. One booted foot rested atop a skull like a trophy, yet his furrowed brow and eyes reflected a sadness that revealed his conscience. The photo showed wear, not just due to age; Grandfather apparently twisted the picture in his hands many times.

She dropped the papers and with shaky fingers gathered the diary into her arms and shoved the photo into the case.

Grandfather fluttered his eyelashes and moved his lips. His fingers grasped at the bed sheet.

She ran out the door with Steve at her heels.

"He's awake," she yelled at the nurses.

The first thing he did when he gained full consciousness was motion her to come closer. He spoke in a voice slurred by his stroke but between her and Steve they understood.

"Did you bury me at Pecos? My heart beats there still because the Pecos is where we began. Life and death should come full circle," he croaked.

"Governor, didn't you hear the doctor? You can't die yet. I'm going to bring home the bones. You have a reunion to look forward to."

In his confusion he must have misunderstood her words. He thrashed about the bed and the attendants tied him down.

He cried something about his rusty magic. "Why does my spirit linger in the crossbow of life?"

3

Four weeks had passed since he returned to the living. Two weeks earlier the hospital moved him to a rehabilitative center. Thanks to stroke therapy, the slur in his voice had lessened until he spoke almost normal.

He sat in a recliner while she combed his white head and braided his hair.

"I've brought you bread baked from my horno oven. I have my oven shaped like a bee hive; you have your bees; together we can make honey bread," she said.

"Your bread does not smell like the cow and the bee as Old-Woman's did. Butter skated across her yeast while honey ruled her rise like a queen. How I miss her legumes and stews. She sat on my lap when I lay in your truck with one moccasin in the grave. Odd, none of my wives floated over to welcome me. I would have married her had she not lost patience and left to look for a dead husband, one more talkative than I," he said, laughing.

"My old honey is still single and wants me. My magic failed else I would be dancing at my wedding right now. There will be no wedding guests. You will regret after my death, that I cannot in clear conscience become one with the Cloud People and float up to Kachina Village, while they are lost," he said, crossing his arms and thrusting out his chin.

"I've wanted to tell you, but your doctor advised me to wait. I've called NAGPRA and we have a right to claim everything Dr. Kidder took from Pecos."

"This man was no kidder but a thief," he said.

"The Pecos land was privately owned in 1915 so he legally stole for science," she said.

"The land is red because of our blood and why Pecos has always belonged to us," he said, spitting and wiping his mouth with a shaky hand.

Hopefully, her news about NAGPRA would calm him down but he swatted her hand away like a fly. She swore not to argue with him and bit her lip.

"Where is Steve? You should be home seeing to your husband," he said.

"He's at work. He has orders to fill. You know what a fine jeweler he is and his turquoise designs are in high demand."

"You are not a good wife."

"I'm trying to be a good granddaughter so I visit every day to make sure you don't frighten the nurses off."

He promised to eat all his dinner but like a child, he turned his mouth away from the spoon she offered.

"Fine, don't eat," she said, stomping out of the room without even a good night.

4

He moped about the house for six weeks and she swore at times he spied on her and eavesdropped on her every conversation. Then suddenly, he set to work like an ant scurrying around a bread crumb.

She spied on him not to be malicious but because of concern for his health.

While washing dishes, she watched him stroll up the dusty trail of Blue Bird Mesa carrying a white owl with an eagle balanced on his shoulder.

She tiptoed to his shed and peeked in the window.

He cut a chunk of coyote fur. Taking needle and thread, he sewed the ends together to form a tube, which he twisted around a tree branch. At the other end of the branch, he twisted rabbit fur, similarly sewn as a tube. He then placed a spell on the branch so the wood would form a circle. He tied the ends together with a strap of leather and attached a buffalo tooth to both the coyote and rabbit fur.

He spun a circular net that resembled a spider's web, him like a tarantula, his humped back rising from his wrinkled neck and working his arthritic fingers like each hand ended in twenty digits with sharp nail-like claws. When he finished, he worked the net through the inside rim of the circular branch and tightened the strings taut as the strings of a bow. He attached to the net an arrowhead, and silver and copper balls. He plucked feathers from the owl and eagle and hung the feathers from the circular branch.

Of course! He created his latest concoction—a dream catcher which is a mystical configuration resembling a handleless tennis racket with a tiny hole in the center.

Lastly, he attached a leather strip to the dream catcher to hang it from above his bed.

A dream catcher was meant to trap nightmares in the web so bad dreams do not get through and invade sleep. At least, good dreams would keep him company while she collected the family bones.

It was a good time to pack for tomorrow's trip while dreams occupied the old man. Steve just arrived with a few friends to help him place the camper shell on her pickup.

After a month of stroke therapy and six weeks on the mend, Grandfather reverted to his sour self so pity Steve's Aunt Faye who moved in to help care for him while she drove to Boston.

Hidden beneath her underwear in her dresser drawer was a photograph, twisted like the picture of the bones, only she was the one who ravished this picture Grandfather never knew she found of her mother who died when she was born. She and her mother looked sort of similar, with the same hollow look in their eyes, except a snake did not physically mark her mother's forehead. A delicate necklace glowed like the sun and hung around her mother's neck. Five tips swirled around a heart protruding in the middle of an unusual silver shape. Perhaps her father had been a jeweler and fashioned this necklace for her mother. She looked everywhere for the necklace, except Grandfather's snake den and beehives, but never found it.

She also possessed a doll made by her mother, carefully packed away in her suitcase, tucked in a zippered pocket for safe keeping.

Jesus! He snuck up on her like always, making her heart jump.

Quick, she hid her mother's picture behind her back and held her breath. Thank goodness he failed to notice her nervousness.

He stood with his fists on his hips, legs spread apart, chin thrust out like a petulant child, ready to throw a temper tantrum.

Aunt Faye cowered behind him, holding an old suitcase tied closed with a rope.

"I am going with you to this Harvard. I don't need taking care of," he said.

"You can't go with me. You've been ill and your age..."

"This is my purpose. It is why Pautiwa would not let me cross the bridge to the other side because I must bring the bones home myself."

"No way," she said.

"All the time I floated in this so-called coma, I visited with Pautiwa. We smoked together and he told me that he sets a table with food for the missing ones. Every night he neglects the others in Kachina Village and eats alone with a table set for thousands. In the morning he must throw the food out. It is such a waste."

"No."

"My going is the only way to retrieve my honor and prove to the bones that I am no coward; though I am feeble, I brave the miles they once did. Else, how can I bang my fork and spoon on the table in Kachina Village? Better to be a dog and hang my head for table scraps. I am going with you," he said, lifting his chin proudly but dullness flattened his eyes.

So that was that.

"Okay, but we're going to fly. I'll sell my truck to pay for the tickets," she said, sighing and lifting her hands in surrender.

"I will not fly under anyone's power but my own."

"Right, and naturally, I can't fly on your back now that you're old."

"You will drive me on my last spirit journey. Before I die, I wish to cross my country and see the ocean on the other side."

"I'll drive you to Boston to claim the bones, but you are not riding on your mattress in the back of my truck, I mean camper since it now has a shell, sorry though it is. You'll ride up front with me. Though it is May, the days might be cool."

"The wind and the sun are not the same as on the path to Pecos so I do not care if I ride in the back on my mattress or beside you."

She felt like a bride, something borrowed, something blue, something new. The shell was borrowed. The blue was her turquoise good-luck ring. The new was her, patient and kind and sweet to Grandfather. She showed her teeth in what could pass as a snarling smile. "No mattress."

The next morning he must have grabbed her truck keys because he sat in the truck with his magic hat leaning jauntily on the side of his head. He straightened the feather best he could but it still hung like a half-ass television antennae made from a clothes hanger. He rested his hands on the ceremonial staff and stared straight ahead at the empty road before him.

He still insisted on taking his mattress. Steve loaded it in the back of the camper.

She jerked her arms into her robe and scurried outside.

"Whoa, Baby, I would not have left for work without kissing you goodbye," Steve said.

"I don't want that thing in my truck."

"Chill out. You'll rest more comfortably in your sleeping bag on the mattress than on the metal of the truck bed. This defiance against the old man has to stop."

"I suppose when you put it that way, the mattress makes sense. I'm really trying with him but he doesn't make it easy," she said.

"I'll miss you," he said.

She nodded her head, too choked up to speak. They would return in a week or two but tears flowed down her cheeks and shocked her when Steve drove away. She normally hid her soft side but the old man's illness upset her equilibrium and the thought of driving so far scared her. Her panic turned to dread of a lecture for having overslept for ten minutes, so she swallowed the eggs and bacon Aunt Faye fixed, dressed in record time and ran out the door, still feeling uptight and not looking forward to a road trip from hell.

She opened the door and lifted her boot to climb up.

"There is a burlap sack in my bedroom. Fetch it," he ordered.

Not even a good morning. How did you sleep? How are you feeling?

She returned his hateful look with a glacier stare of her own before marching back to the house. When she exited the house, the front door slammed behind her, letting him know that was her last trip to his room.

"What's in the bag," she said, frowning at the burlap sack and shaking it.

"Put my sack in the back. Drive me to this Boston." His tone ordered her to shut up and mind her own business. The wind slapped his greasy white braids across her cheek and the odor of a rattlesnake egg shell, mixed with raw honey from his beehives, assaulted her nose. He always combined sweetness with poison. His recent illness did not transform him into the gentle grandfather she hoped would materialize. If anything, he was even more ornery than before and demanded they stop at Pecos to begin their journey.

"It's out of our way, Governor. I want to make Oklahoma City before sunset."

"I must commune with the ghosts and tell them we are going to bring home the bones."

She couldn't help herself and laughed at the stupidity of it all. They traveled with a ratty camper. His smelly mattress served as a bed. They also brought along an old camping stove, blankets and pillows, a five-gallon water tank, food cooler and folding chairs. She prayed her money would last.

"I don't know how you get me into these things," she mumbled, thinking of her boss' astonished face when he learned of her cross-country drive to pick up a couple thousand skeletons, after a stop at D.C. to show a certificate of authenticity that proved she and Grandfather were the last of the Pecos. Getting the proof together did not go so smoothly, especially working with the closed-mouthed old coot who sat beside her. At least her boss said her job as a slot supervisor at the San Felipe Hollywood Casino would be waiting for her.

She knew how to get a rise out of the old man and nudged him with her elbow. "Once we declare our legitimacy as the last Pecos survivors, we should file to open a casino, get some revenge against the white man by robbin' his pockets for all that blood that drip-dripped down the mountains," she said.

"You wish to defile our homeland with gambling invaders?"

"I actually thought a casino is like a trade fair. You once told me Pecos was the crossroads of the world where they held prosperous trade fairs and Spanish invaders and Plains Indians came to buy and sell, along with the other pueblos. We can even make a casino of tipis like they did to trade their money for fun at the slots."

Her attempt to dignify her joke did not amuse him. For the remainder of the drive he sulked like an unhappy camper probably because for the first time in her life she laughed at him instead of with him. Ever since he almost died, he no longer seemed so frightening. Instead, he was pitiful because of his damned old age, but at least he would live to see his dream of the stolen bones reburied at Pecos.

They arrived at the ruins, her in a better mood than last time. He wobbled, pounding the ground with the ceremonial staff and clinging to her elbow. Their path was difficult to maneuver since she dragged his burlap sack behind her. At least the sucker wasn't heavy, just cumbersome.

A rattlesnake slithered across their path and he stopped to let it pass while she muffled her screams with her hand.

Her vivid memories caused the scar on her forehead to ache. She remembered herself as a skinny seven-year-old girl with an unscarred forehead, darker skinned than now. Spring bloomed but given the Jemez altitude and the sun's brutality, the earth overheated. Two long braids roped into a bun on her head so the sun kissed her neck; the sun god loved her and did not burn her but caressed her with its warm rays. Even at the age of seven, she had a sensuous nature and heavy lidded eyes. Her friends teased about her bedroom eyes which made her look like she was dreaming. Wide-eyed that day, she balanced her toes at the ledge of a snake den.

The snakes purred at her, their hissing sounding like an invitation. The eyes of the largest snake hypnotized her.

Suddenly, something clawed her neck, jerked her back from the den and made her airborne then set her roughly on the ground.

She spun in a fit of temper, but no one was there.

Then, as if he projected from thin air, Grandfather stood on the other side of the snake den. He must have walked over from their shack hidden by hills and trees some distance behind him.

He stood like a barrel with both fists on his hips. He yelled and accused her of following him, after he strictly forbade her to leave the house.

She screamed back at him for scaring her; "I know nothing about your stupid secret snake den!"

Her words wobbled in the air because he shook her until her teeth rattled.

He pinched her neck, marching her to their shabby house, her fists flying out, trying to strike him.

Thus, on her seventh birthday she sat in her bedroom and cried, not because of some dumb old snakes. If he knew snakes didn't scare her, he might slap her silly. She cried because he ripped the collar of her new dress when he dragged her away. Old-Woman, who cooked and cleaned for them, sewed the dress for her birthday. She disliked Old-Woman, but the dress was her new favorite in the entire world and deserved a grunt of a thank you when Old-Woman handed her the gift. Old-Woman offered a wrinkled cheek, and she took a step back. Old-Woman held out her hand, and her own hand hung limp at her side.

Old-Woman's sewing skill was admirable, but her face was too ugly to look at. Rather, she stared at the sparse hairs on her chin and often referred to her as Bearded-Lady to her friends. All the girls laughed at her imitation of Old-Woman swaying her wide hips in front of Grandfather and waving her butt in his face.

She refused to address Old-Woman by her given name. It was easy to ignore his sometimes-companion, except on those nights when with her hands cuffed to her ears, she could not drown out moans and grunts coming from the other side of the thin walls.

The sun now set in the scene from her past and silence echoed from the shack. She lay on her bed in the fetus position and hugged her damaged birthday dress. In the dusk a chair was barely visible in her bedroom. Three crooked shelves hung from the wall. One shoe teetered on the edge of the lower shelf because she had thrown her shoes at the wall in a temper tantrum when he ordered her to bed early, not even fried bread with honey for her seventh birthday.

The smell of baked bread wafted in from the horno oven outside her window and tortured her. Grandfather should have nicknamed her Hollow-Stomach instead of Hollow-Woman which she hated, such an adult name for a girl. He told her he named her Hollow-Woman because a motherless girl would have to grow up fast.

Moisture gathered at the corners of her eyes and her lip trembled at a noise. Maybe he forgave her and brought her a birthday gift.

Something slithered across her bed. She could feel the object's weight crawl along her ankle and across her knee.

The last rays of the sun shone through her window and illuminated the head of a snake, its tail rattling on her calf. The snake king that earlier stared at her with such interest had crawled from the snake den to her room. She didn't know whether to feel scared or honored.

Before she could decide, the snake struck her in the center of her forehead right between her eyes.

Grandfather seemed to leap from the air and materialize in her bedroom. He grabbed the snake before it could strike again. He let out what sounded like a strangled scream and yanked off the snake's head.

She lay paralyzed on her bed with her nose pointed up. The headless body of the snake wiggled in her lap, the tail whipping about her head causing her forehead to swell. She tasted vomit on her lips.

Vaguely aware of Grandfather, the pungent odor of burning herbs teased her nostrils and his warm breath gave her scant comfort. Through a fog, she heard a sucking sound and then spits, followed by the pressure of his thumbs as he worked poison from her head. Her head felt big, then small...big, then small. It seemed he intended to suck the very brains from her skull.

Her last thought before losing consciousness was that it would serve him right if she died.

She woke to sunlight and her head resting in his lap. He held a glass of goat milk to her lips and she sipped.

He watched her closely and gave her a rare smile because she managed to hold the milk down.

"You shouldn't have revealed yourself to the snakes, little One. The snakes claimed your father for their own when he sought their poison to end his sadness at losing your mother."

The softness of his voice surprised her. She suddenly felt shy. They never really had a grown-up conversation before. Usually he grunted or snapped impatiently at her, or she screamed at him in fits of temper. Their conversations usually ended with him smacking her lightly on the back of the head, or pulling on her braids, and scolding her for being so much like him...too much like him

"Tell me more about my father, happy things."

"He killed himself because your mother died after giving birth to you."

He seemed not to notice the shock he gave her. She never put two and two together before that her parents' deaths was her fault. She doubled over and vomited.

While he calmly skinned the snake, she wrinkled her nose and moved to the corner of her bed, away from her would-be murderer, the king snake.

"Do not dread the snakes. Our brothers know you are one of them because we belong to the Snake Clan. I've moved my snake den to a place where you will not find them. I am heavy with sadness that I have killed my brother the snake. The Ridge-nosed Rattlesnake is an endangered species, as you and I are," he said.

"What's an endangered species?" she said.

"The Ridge-nosed snakes are becoming extinct. They are such magnificent creatures to vanish from this land and proud warriors. Too bad their breed is dying out."

She opened her eyes wide because it never occurred to her that he might die. He was old, but then he must have been born old, wise, and all-seeing. Everyone they ever came across treated him with utmost respect and a little fear. He was invincible; he could never die. She must not let Grandfather see her fright. He was not as similar to her as he thought. She could never embody a snake; snakes are fearless.

It was then he told her, "Our Pecos Pueblo is a place so magical, our holy serpent sleeps hidden in a cave nearby, waiting for his worshippers to return. Alas, snakes have no outer ears and just you and I jumping upon the earth and pounding drums cannot make a noise loud enough to wake him. In over a hundred years he has not forged any new arroyos as he snakes across the ground, so I know he has not left his cave. He is lazy, that one."

"A monster snake?" she said.

"Do not fret; the snakes are our elder brothers; stay away from the snakes else they might jealously claim you as their own and snatch you from me."

He rubbed a paste on her forehead, which cooled the pain from her snakebite and soothed her. The paste seemed to soak into her brain so she felt bubbly and warm.

"But you don't leave the snakes alone, Governor," she said with a slurred voice, sounding like she lived in a cave.

"I have frolicked with them so the snakes do as I bid. I have searched all these years for the feathered serpent of Pecos, yet he eludes me, so I chase the rattlers and other snakes in hope that in the breed born this year lives the feathered serpent, but so far all the eggs have hatched small and bald."

She stared with wide eyes at the king snake. He searched for a giant snake?

He lifted his braid from his neck and showed her his own snake scar.

And so she discovered on her seventh birthday that the feathered serpent from Pecos always marked the Snake Clan as his very own. This discovery was followed by several years spent running after Grandfather, chasing the feathered serpent until her legs outgrew his and she led the chase. Finally, at the age of twelve, she stopped running. Twenty-three years passed since then and the ruins deteriorated even more but the hopeless trails were still visible where she snaked across on wild goose chases.

He, however, never gave up and Steve drove him to Pecos occasionally; and Grandfather hung his head, dog-like, from the window while they drove around, looking for snake trails.

"In all these years, have you ever seen even a glimpse of the feathered serpent, Governor?" she now said.

"You grew up and matured into a weak woman. I longed for a grandson but perhaps one day you will find the cave at Pecos where the feathered serpent of the Aztecs sleeps and the Snake Clan will not become extinct," he said, leaning the ceremonial staff against the jagged wall of the church ruins. He touched her shoulder but she shrugged him off and stared at the ground—anywhere but at him.

"Do not fret, because it is not your fault Moctezuma cursed the Pecos Pueblo centuries ago. I blame myself, Granddaughter, because you have no son."

"Yes, I know." She waved her truck keys in his face. A tiny figure of Kokopelli swung from her fingers.

"Do not mock the old ways," he said.

He gifted her with the key chain on her wedding day. Kokopelli, Casanova of the Cliff Dwellers, had a hump on his back filled with male seed. Kokopelli visited the pueblos, playing his flute in warm spring;

evening stars would dance to his music. Come morning, crops flourished and life stirred within the wombs of women at the pueblo.

Her marriage begat a dozen years of sorcery and modern procreation techniques all meant to torture her. She believed all these years he blamed her because the babies she carried slipped from her womb too young to live, frail like herself, miserable like herself. But all this time he held back from her like he always did, even as he shrank with age.

"You should have explained sooner that it is not my fault I am weak," she said.

"I didn't want to scare you," he said, and then frightened the bejesus out of her. "You are cursed, Granddaughter, and I fear for your future."

"Well I've got many years left, I hope."

He puffed on a hand-rolled cigarette, blowing smoke in her exasperated face. He yanked open the burlap sack and jerked out a two-foot hand-carved statue of a Franciscan friar with Bible open, upon which sat a baby statue. A halo of hair encircled the monk's bald scalp.

"What's this, Governor?"

"The idol is St. Anthony of Padua, patron saint of barren women."

"You shouldn't waste what little money you have on miracles," she said pressing against her empty womb.

He shoved the statue at her then pulled from his bag of tricks the dream catcher he had made.

"As you know, a dream catcher sifts dreams and visions. The first morning rays melt the nightmares that have been caught. The small hole in the center allows good dreams to pass through and make sleep pleasant. The webbing is for strength and the feathers are the whisperings of the spirit. I've made this dream catcher special for you, Granddaughter."

Touched, she reached out her hand but he yanked his gift from her reach.

"I now make this dream catcher something you have never seen before."

He grabbed his ceremonial pipe from his knapsack. The pipe was about a foot long and decorated with glass beads. Striped wool bands covered half the pipe. Silk ribbons of various colors adorned the pipe, intermixed with horsehair.

He shoved his pipe between his lips, and she flipped open her cigarette lighter, returning his dirty look. Yeah. So what? The hypocrite often yelled at her to quit smoking, but the calm of a cigarette lessened the stresses of her life. Now the burden of one day being the last of a dying species gave her the heebie-jeebies.

"When another vision came to me of my death," he said, puffing on his pipe, "I began to make this death gift for you. I finished the dream catcher this morning."

He lifted the dream catcher in the air and waved the net around. He blew sacred smoke through the net and sang in their native tongue, Towa.

"With this dream catcher I ensnare my people's history," he said in a thundering voice, raising his arms to the sky.

"You have been sleeping and waiting for the stolen ones to join you once again. Now you must help my granddaughter find her family for she is as lost as the missing ones." He blew on his flageolet fashioned from a bird's bone so the music of his flute instrument sounded like a canary. With haunting notes, he called forth Pecos spirits who rose from their graves. Mists of cold air steamed from the ground and entered the dream catcher's net. The feathers of the dream catcher fluttered, and whisperings came from the owl and the eagle feathers. An eerie fog formed and spelled out her name. The letters evaporated into the netting, as if to brand it. The net pushed out as a fist shoved through its center, then retracted with a whoosh and the dream catcher hung silent and still.

"I made this dream catcher special. If the net spins clockwise then nightmares are trapped and good dreams pass through, but if the net spins counter, nightmares spellbind your sleep."

Oh, God, not again. He scared her so much she whimpered and bit her nails.

"Be silent. You must learn not just the happiness of Pecos but the sadness and terror of your people. Your journey must be spiritual as well as physical, and with the promise of finding your family, perhaps, you will even discover yourself. When you find the bones (Did she imagine a threat in his voice?) your curse of barrenness will lift and the Pecos will flourish once more."

"You don't play fair, Governor," she said, turning her back to him. She could never describe her emptiness because he was her only family, and they differed in body and soul. Just desolation and death lingered at Pecos, like her empty womb.

She dug her toe into the ground, ready to sprint, and he grabbed her shoulder, spun her around and pinched her.

"Here is your family, my final gift to you," he said.

She reached out a shaky hand and grabbed one end of the dream catcher and they tugged between them.

He appeared crazed and his eyes wild.

Finally, he let go and with two fingers, she held out her gift with distaste, a dream catcher made not to spin dreams of sugar clouds and peppermints but to spin darkness and fill her dreams with nightmares.

With a heavy heart, she threw her dream catcher in the back of the camper and wondered if peace would ever come between them.

As he rode silently beside her towards I-40, she dreaded the next couple of weeks with the two of them confined in her truck like two battering horned buffalos.

It should be enough she kept her promise.

It was too much the Pecos ruins turned her life topsy-turvy, if even for two weeks.

Well, she never gave her word about loving any of those bones that needed rescuing, and no dreams or nightmares could ever force her.

How odd, he fashioned a dream catcher to teach her about the ancestors, yet he rarely spoke about her mother and father.

The bleak ruins shrunk behind her in the rearview mirror. Clouds followed and she pushed harder on the gas pedal, just in case some of those restless spirits felt comforted today and transformed into cloud people. Pecos ghosts traveled with them in that damned dream catcher. She didn't need any cloud people stalking her.

5

"I-40 is a historic route. Well, not exactly, but the two-lane road that runs alongside is the old Route 66. I guess you could say the road connected New Mexico to the rest of the country in the 1920's. During the depression migrants with possessions piled atop their cars, drove west across Route 66, escaping the great Dust Bowl, looking for work. Did you ever travel any of the routes in the old days?" she said.

"Bah! I do not steer my horse along paths set by others but forge my own way. Other's travails do not depress me because I mind my own business. I have my own dust to contend with and it is not so great. What about the Indian trails or should I say trials? Are they not historic enough for you?"

"Governor, are you sure...? We're getting close to the state line. You look tired."

"Want some fruit?" he said.

"I can still drive you back to Jemez."

"I would rather die here in your truck than bear to watch the dust of the road take you far away, Granddaughter."

His words touched her so much; she about choked on a piece of apple.

"Besides, how can I entrust the bones to such a stupid woman?" he said.

She gripped the steering wheel tighter and forgot to offer him a nap on his mattress.

They didn't quite make Oklahoma City but stayed at Red Rock Canyon State Park located off 281. Other travelers claimed all the picnic tables so they sat on the tailgate and ate, him swinging his short legs beside her like a child.

After feasting on Aunt Faye's beans, fried chicken and corn on the cob, she built a fire, unfolded a chair for him and covered his shoulders with his blanket.

She dropped to her feet, snuggled against his legs, and opened Alfred Kidder's diary.

She imagined a thirty-year-old antiquities hound sitting in his tent dressed like in the picture, in standard gear of a 1915 archeologist. Tan khaki pants flared out at his hips. Boots planted firmly in Pecos dust. Sleeves of his tan khaki shirt rolled up. Wide brimmed hat pushed back on his sweating forehead and wisps of hair sticking out of the crown. Spectacles halfway down his thin nose. He chewed a pipe he forgot to light. He bent over a makeshift desk scribbling in his diary.

"March 1, 1915.

In the desert-like landscape of New Mexico, I have discovered the ruins of the Pecos Indians. For over six hundred years these Indians lived scattered about in mud and rock villages. Then some time in the Fourteenth Century the natives left these five or six villages and united to form the Pecos Pueblo, which by 1450 they constructed into an extraordinary complex of four and five story buildings built in a terrace structure. Imagine thousands of rooms under one roof nearly two centuries before the Mayflower landed at Plymouth Rock. Not bad for savages."

Grandfather scoffed and she kept reading.

"Pecos Indians were among the first North Americans to come in contact with Europeans and a different way of life. My historian tells me there are Spanish documents in Santa Fe written by a visitor in 1591 who describes the apartments here which housed a couple of thousand Indians. The visitor must have been with the illegal Gaspar Castaño de Sosa expedition. Like other Spanish expeditions before him, the Spaniards demanded food and clothing from the Pecos Indians and punished them for not complying. There were probably some public hangings and kiva burnings before the Spanish sacked the pueblo for whatever they could find of any worth. The Spaniards always looked for precious metals but found none.

The Pecos Indians must have chosen to build on this high rocky ridge for self-defense and to look out over the green valley at the southern end of the Sangre de Cristo Mountains. From here they could see down below any approaching plains Indians not as civilized as they."

The word, civilized, satisfied Grandfather and he nodded his agreement. He motioned with his hand to continue reading.

"There is a stream on each side of the ridge. I imagine they fished from the Pecos River which is a little over a mile away.

We are currently digging for any adobe buildings, once four and five stories high, but all we find are jagged walls and the remains of but one story. Centuries of wind pushing against the adobe walls, and rains and snow washing away a bit of mud each year, have taken its toll so we feel lucky to have found anything at all left of the buildings. Jack found a broken ladder once used to climb from story to story as one pulls the ladder up and then reuses the ladder to climb to the next story and so on. It's difficult at times to distinguish what was actually part of the pueblo buildings since the Indians utilized the sun-baked mud to build their apartments and any lumber they used disintegrated with the elements. Damn sun is so strong the rays penetrate a man's head until his brain sponges and sweat pours down his shirt.

We've killed many rattlers in this area and as bad luck would have it, a snake bit my servant, who lay gravely ill before expiring, so I always wear my boots. I hired a local English-speaking native to replace my servant, Peters, who worked for me five years. The man is Navajo and we have a communication problem but yet we manage. He's a hard worker and I must confess Peters was a bit lazy."

She could see the diary upset Grandfather.

"I will read more when you are not so tired, Governor," she said, patting his knee.

"It is because of this thief that the Ridge-nosed snake is endangered."

"The archaeologist killing a few snakes eighty-four years ago would not have made the Ridge-nosed extinct today."

"Bah," he said, walking off to use the bathroom.

"Take the flashlight," she yelled.

"I can see with the eyes of an owl. What uses have I for your artificial ways?"

Nevertheless she pointed the flashlight at his back and did not breathe easy until he returned on his wobbly legs, smelling a bit like piss.

He smacked her hand offered him for help to climb into the camper bed.

His snores sounded as mean as him.

She plopped down on the chair and wrapped his blanket around her shoulders. This was the same blanket she knitted for him, the one he kept all these years. Did he save the raggedy blanket out of sentimentality or thrift? Most likely, he kept the blanket same as he kept that ancient hat of his. He had always been dirt poor, his only riches worthless relics and those damned stolen bones, precious ivory to him. He cared so much for the bones that jealousy stirred within her. She brooded into the fire and remembered the morning after her seventh birthday and snake bite.

"Come," Grandfather had said.

He gripped her hand and helped her to rise from bed and dress. He let her stuff her mouth with all the bread and honey she wanted and drink two glasses of goat milk.

He bundled her in his truck and drove, zigzagging down the back roads and highways since he had cataracts in both eyes, was seventy-two years old, and did not drive so well.

He slammed on the brakes and she landed on the truck floor.

She reached her head up like the snakes in his den and made a face because they stopped at some ugly old pile of rocks and raggedy walls and holes in the earth.

"This is our home, the Pecos Pueblo. I brought you at the age of three but you do not remember. It is time you learn more about where you come from," he said.

"I hate this place and won't ever live here, even if you make me," she said and stamped her foot.

His eyes looked as desolate as the rubble, so she patted him on the knee to comfort him.

"There are no roofs to protect us from the rain, Governor. Just a few zigzag walls. The buildings aren't done."

He yanked open the door, grabbed her arm and dragged her from the truck. He shook her, though more gently than on her birthday, mindful of the red and raw scar on her forehead.

"Has the snake poisoned your brain? This land is the ruins of our family. Only you and I are left," he shouted.

"I'm not an endangered species," she screamed, kicking at his snakeskin boots planted bow-legged in the earth.

He picked her up and hugged her so tightly his heart stilled, and the same coldness froze her own heart so it seemed they were already dead, her and the old man. They slithered among the ruins like two Pecos ghosts.

He carried her to his truck with her face buried in his shoulder. She inflated her nostrils and sniffed. He bathed once a month and never during the winter months, but he always smelled of stinky horse, sweet beehives, and spices, the herbs of a medicine chief intermixed with Old Spice Aftershave, his only nod to vanity. His was a heady scent of artistry and masculinity.

She hugged him tighter around his neck and squeezed his whitish-grey ponytail, smiling at his discomfort.

He set her gently down on the passenger seat, and grinned.

He wasn't mad at her but by the time the seat leather creaked on his side of the truck; a wrinkle furrowed her brow because his smile had been secretive.

She shifted her eyes two generations across from her to a bona fide prehistoric Indian, the real thing, not one of them bored wooden statues lounging outside a cigar store. A filthy bandanna kept his shoulder length, greasy hair neatly framing his weather-beaten face. His hair was the color of iron-grey, like a choo-choo train, making him appear like he was going places, if only he could see where he was going. His eyes appeared crazed and his cataracts made him look like an alien. They would never bridge the gap separating them, he of the old Indian ways and the crumbling Pecos Pueblo, while she longed to be a modern 1971 child and lusted after her own television set, and all the wonders of a world outside the reservation.

Usually he chugged down the interstate about twenty-five miles per hour but he now drove recklessly, fish tailing across I-25 like a trout. He clenched the steering wheel with white fists and thrust out his chin. With heavy wrinkled eyelids it seemed he drove with his eyes closed guided by an Indian ancestor, one born before cars were invented. The pickup swerved in and out of traffic, crossing yellow lines before swinging back over to the shoulder, barely missing the moving targets. The pickup backfired, exploding like Fourth of July fireworks or serial farts after a satisfying meal of pinto beans. When the pickup missed, sparks flew from the exhaust.

Her right hand grabbed the window frame and her left hand grasped the torn seat. She hung on for dear life, the wind blowing her hair about her face, and feeling very much alive. See. She was not Hollow-Woman, even if it did take the excitement of a wild ride to make her heart beat. The ancient family ruins drooped behind them, looking forlorn, and just to be ornery she threw a dirty finger at the back window of the truck.

His body stiffened.

Ha-ha! He would never mold her into what he wanted. She was too much like him, a free spirit stamped with a snake's fierce pride, and stubborn as a wild animal captured but never tamed.

"Governor, I'm hungry."

He refused to look at her. He hunkered lower in his seat and glared at the road.

A beastly grunt came from him and she accused him of farting.

He jerked the steering wheel at the Santa Fe exit and cursed.

Good. Her mouth watered and she rubbed her stomach, squeezing her eyes tight, crossing her fingers and wishing he would buy her a hamburger like the one she licked in a magazine.

He swung the truck right and skidded into a parking lot. Instead of a hamburger sign, the words, St. Mary's Boarding School for Indians, screamed back at her. She swallowed her appetite and bile rose to her throat. A hollow feeling emptied her stomach so her belly button touched her spine. She turned in her seat and stared out the back window, and watched with wide eyes him yank a worn suitcase from the truck bed.

She jumped down from the truck, clung to his legs, and begged him not to leave her at the school. She would be good. She would not look for snakes. She would not throw dirty fingers again. She would stop cussing. She would never smoke a cigarette again nor would she ever beg for a taste of wine. She promised to go back to Pecos and live with him in the ruins with the ghosts, and the feathered serpent, and the blood, and the witches, and the headless priests.

"But please, please don't leave me here all alone in this strange place."

"Governor, please come back."

"Come back!"

"Grandfather," she pleaded.

"I'm sorry I killed my parents!"

When his dust cloud cleared, he was gone like in those cowboys-and-Indians movies where the hero rides off in the sunset. He had given her a gift for her seventh birthday after all, the gift of living apart from him during the school months with nuns dressed in bad habits, black material swatting against thick ankles as they lifted rulers and brought the metal down upon her knuckles and the backs of her legs. The words the nuns screamed hurt more: heathen, granddaughter of a witch, snake girl, spawn of the devil, spoiled brat. We'll beat the evil out of you, Girl.

She cussed and screamed at the ladies-in-black that, I am a witch.

The nuns shivered and crossed themselves, except for the meanest one, Sister Catherine, who once brought a large metal crucifix down upon her head and gave her a slight concussion.

She suffered a headache, a black out and then a wake up in the infirmary where the man with sad eyes, hanging on a cross, stared back at her and then she had some stuttering to do. She didn't really mean anything against Him but fumed at his servants. She hardly even knew Him but hated Grandfather for leaving her with the nuns because she didn't want to live at his ghost pueblo. Nights of crying into her pillow, days of watching for his truck, Grandfather was the master of broken promises.

So why in heaven's name was she here, years later, at Red Rock Canyon keeping her promise to him?

She sat hunched by the fire, hugging that same suitcase, only a rope now held it together. She choked on memories of St. Mary's until embers turned to cold ashes. She hated the bones and struggled not to resent an old man set in his ways and unable to ever change. He was who he was, and she didn't know who the hell she was, the nuns saw to that.

She wearily climbed into the camper and fell on the booze-stained mattress, scooting as far to the left edge as possible. Naturally, he would claim the right, just like his smell made the camper his own. Tobacco, wine, horses, sweat and grease clogged her nose.

I miss Steve and my own bed, my job, even my boring routine.

She spoke to Steve earlier without saying, I love you; I miss you. She took after the old man, stubborn, demanding, insisting on having her own way, manipulative. Sometimes she wondered if Grandfather gave Steve a love potion so that he would fall in love with her.

Moonlight shone in from a camper window and illuminated the ceiling. The dream catcher's shadow spun above her. The old buzzard must have hung it from the ceiling while she stared into the flames, wanting to avoid him and waiting for him to sleep soundly.

Her eyes grew heavy as her dream catcher twirled around like a pocket watch dangling from the hand of a hypnotist. The dream catcher spun clockwise and glowed in the dark, growing brighter with each 360 degree turn.

With each spin a mist blew from the net and covered the camper until a fog enveloped her.

The smell of damp earth filled her nostrils and paralysis engulfed her limbs. She was awake, yet not awake, seeing, yet dreaming. One nostril filled with mud; her other nostril had only a pinhole for air. She sank fast into the soft earth. If lack of air didn't kill her, panic would.

Through the fog appeared visions…the ruins of the Pecos Pueblo beneath a grey sky.

Bones rattled and the earth shook.

From the Pecos dirt, skeletons formed as part of the natural landscape; ribs protruded from dust; skulls appeared like mounds of anthills; bony feet popped through the earth.

Thunder cracked in the sky. Lightning scorched the ground, striking across their skulls. Like Frankenstein come to life, the skeletons' ribs moved up and down.

Skeletons pushed through their graves, stood on bony feet and shook off the dust. There must have been a couple thousand skeletons staggering amongst the pueblo ruins.

The clouds moved northward and the sky lightened. The skeletons turned their skulls to the sun.

A mighty wind blew covering the ruins and skeletons with dust. The taste of dirt sickened her stomach and the wind blew her about, so she moved restlessly on the mattress.

Dust whirled, blowing the covers off, leaving her shivering, and clearing the air so at last, she could breathe. Her mattress lay in the center of a large plaza, surrounded by ceremonial kivas. Swirling dirt dampened to mud and plastered itself to stones until a quadrangle of apartment-like buildings formed on an enormous rock.

A ladder appeared and her nightgown blew around her ankles as she lifted her hands from rung to rung and climbed from the camper to the second story of one of the adobe buildings. She heaved herself up the opening big enough for just one person.

The architects had laid out houses in back-to-back blocks. Each story had pathways around all the houses. She walked around the entire second story, using a pathway built like a wooden street with covered protection from the rain.

Dragging the ladder from rooftop to rooftop, she used the ladder as one would a staircase. On the fifth and final story, a comforting breeze blew her hair, cooling her neck, as she stood at the top of the Pecos world. Visible from here were streams nourishing crops of beans, squash and corn cultivated along Glorieta Creek.

There existed two sets of apartment-like buildings constructed as quadrangles—a north complex and a south complex. Each apartment contained about sixteen rooms divided into five floors, all whitewashed, each neatly kept. The pueblo, big enough to house several thousand, was one impressive, massive unit connected by bridges and exterior pathways that zigzagged around the levels like streets.

The rectangular hollow of the south complex had a huge plaza containing round pits with underground ceremonial kivas, all designed for different purposes, but each containing the hole Shipapu which connects man to his beginnings.

Indians climbed from the kivas, no longer skeletons but flesh and blood. Women wore blankets tied at their shoulders or in some cases, cloaks made from turkey feathers. Some men adorned their blankets with buffalo hides. She blushed at the cloth covering their private parts.

Fresh water flowed from a spring inside the pueblo.

Farmers removed tools from the ground floors.

Women stored grains.

The gods blessed the pueblo because she overheard them say the storage bins bulged with a three-year food supply. They piled firewood in high columns, along with building timber.

A man created jewelry from turquoise and her heart wrenched because he reminded her of Steve.

Several women made pottery. Others ground corn and flour using a hand stone in circular motions over a grindstone. The odor of steaming tamales and baking bread filled the air.

From rooftop to rooftop, wooden bridges connected the buildings and there were five plazas in all. At the extreme end of a bridge someone bathed. She spun on her toes and nearly stumbled in her haste to get away. She sneaked over to the other end of the pueblo and peeked at another waterhole but luckily no one occupied this one.

People lived on the upper floors and her heart twisted at the sound of crying babies and children laughing.

She peeked into one kitchen and a woman doled out breakfast cereal to bright-eyed children, handing them bowls containing ground blue corn with hot water. Another woman rolled tortillas. The women abundantly supplied the kitchen with herbs and green vegetables. Glazed pottery bowls adorned the room.

She ran breathless to the other side of the roof and looked down below where a wall protected the pueblo. The wall stretched across both sets of the quadrangular apartment buildings. She counted approximately five-hundred well-muscled warriors who scanned the countryside for any enemies who dared approach. The Pecos Pueblo appeared like a fortress with bows and arrows, war clubs, spears and shields stored along these high tiers.

Tension rippled across the warriors as they scanned an approaching party about three times their number, including captured Tiwa slaves. Obviously superior in the party, rode a few hundred Spanish Conquistadors on horseback, accompanied on foot by a Franciscan friar who from what she recalled of New Mexico history, made the invaders legal in the eyes of Catholic Spain. Above all else, infidels must be evangelized and their souls saved.

The warriors marveled at the iron men who rode on animals never before seen by the Pecos. They oohed and ahed over black men who marched with them.

From her history lessons, it was apparent the man riding in front wearing a plumed helmet and golden armor was the Spanish explorer Francisco Vasquez de Coronado. In his right hand he carried his banner which bore his coat of arms.

She opened her mouth to assure the Indians the animals are merely horses and the men not made of iron but wear a mail coat to shield their hearts. Man and horse are not one mythical being but the quilted cotton armor of the horse only makes it seem so. The other strange animals are sheep and cattle. That is cannon the black men pull behind them. The shining man riding so proudly in front is on a fool's quest to find Quivira and the Seven Cities of Gold.

Don't be frightened, she tried to yell. They are men like you. They bleed. They die. They wound.

The black men are slaves...quick, hide the children. Don't let them harm the babies. Don't let them separate the children from their mothers. Don't let them do to you what they did to the Tiwas, burn them at the stake or enslave them. See. There are Tiwas with Coronado, their wrists bound.

But she could only mouth her words as the sun melted the flesh from the warriors until hundreds of skeletons now stood on the roofs, their bows aimed at the approaching Spanish, their brittle bones no match for the armor of the Conquistadors, their arrows toothpicks compared to the Spanish firesticks, the famed harquebus, the latest in 1540 firepower.

Your spears cannot penetrate armor. Rocks and slingshots are no match for the mighty catapult which can hurl boulders. Shields are no protection from cannon; war clubs are useless on Spanish helmets. See the dents on Coronado's helmet made by your fellow Zunis. But her warnings hung silently in the air.

The party stopped marching and Coronado cuffed his mouth with his hands and he yelled up at the pueblo walls.

The warriors scratched their heads in puzzlement.

She could understand no better than the warriors his Spanish words.

A Franciscan friar hammered a large cross into the ground at the foot of the pueblo, while beside him a soldier played the trumpet and others fired their harquebuses into the air.

The final pound of the friar's hammer jolted her back to the camper and her mattress. The dream catcher began to spin and she sighed with relief at the clockwise direction.

There it was still, whisperings, only this time a smattering of Spanish intermixed with the Tiwa and Towa languages.

The dream catcher changed directions and spun counter-clock-wise and the whisperings turned to screams.

Was it her imagination or did a mist cover the camper?

It seemed Grandfather did indeed bring Pecos ghosts with them.

She glared at her dream catcher. Enough for one night! I have to drive tomorrow.

The spinning stopped.

6

The next morning she felt in better spirits and so did the old man. He gave a short grunt and pounded a fork and spoon against the picnic table but his eyes sparkled.

She suspected he knew about her dream and tried hard to keep his mouth shut.

"In Coronado's time the people called our pueblo Cicuye," he blurted out.

"Did they, Governor?"

She conversed with him affectionately over breakfast.

He even helped her clean up, throwing the paper plates in the garbage can, a tradition he normally called woman's work.

They drove out from the campground, still in an amiable mood.

"I have a surprise for you, Governor," she said, rolling her eyes at him.

In Oklahoma City she merged onto I-44 and maneuvered the truck over to the National Cowboy Hall of Fame and parked.

They entered the building and the glass room where a statue of *The End of the Trail* stood.

They stared silently up at the white sculpture of a horsed Native American, slumped over his weary horse, slugging along towards surrender.

"It says here that the sculptor, James Earle Fraser, finished the statue in 1915," she said.

"So the year the thief stole the bones, this man fashioned for all time the agony of defeat in stone. Ah, agony of the soul is eighteen feet tall and weighs four tons. I am not surprised."

"The statue is not made of stone, Governor, it is plaster."

"This Indian belonged to a healing society," he said, pointing at the giant white medicine bag. "Of what pueblo did he come from?"

"He represents all the plains Indians."

"Ah, like our friends the Apache."

"It appears the wind pushes him towards his destiny," she said.

"The destiny of the Indian did not include defeat until the white man stuck his nose in our business and muscled in. All this suffering for the white man's gold," he said.

"And the lust for land," she added.

"I feel small with such tall pain before me but I can relate. Some may think the wanderers suffered more than the pueblos because the invaders did not push us from our lands, but our Spanish conquerors kept coming, one after another with their various punishments. They, too, searched for gold and when they found no precious metals, they mined the Puebloans."

It brought tears to his eyes when he recalled the story told him by his friend Joe Yellowhorse about an ancestor from Acoma Pueblo who had to be dragged around on a blanket because he had but one foot. The Spanish may have cut off his foot but not his tongue, as generation to generation handed down the story of how in 1598, Spain replaced the conquistadors with a pacifier, Don Juan de Oñate, first colonial governor of New Spain Province of New Mexico. He was like a feudal king, issuing commands from his adobe palace.

"This Oñate led Franciscan friars, colonists, and soldiers to the promised land of the Puebloans. The Promised Land, the sun baked valley of the Río Grande, belonged to the Summer People who emerged from Shipapu, yet Oñate claimed for the Spanish king everything, including the Puebloans. He is the man who named our pueblo Pecos and impressed our people with the pageantry of knights. He staged a mock battle at Pecos of the Moors defeat against the Christians. Moors fighting with spears and Spaniards blasting them with harquebuses, like a turkey shoot, blinded our people to the truth. I hear Oñate was addicted to laxative pills, so perhaps he had a conscience. Because of Spanish rifles, the Puebloans had no choice but to welcome the intruders and bow to their whips.

"This man from Acoma, related to Joe, was not always an animal who had to crawl on all fours, but once a warrior. A man's pride shined in his eyes when in 1605 he joined his friends to hurl several vigilante soldiers from the mesa top at the Sky City of Acoma. The soldiers had demanded a double food tax and had roamed Acoma stealing water, wood, clothing, and food, and would have left the pueblo to starve for the winter. The friars declared a just and legal war for the Spanish to retaliate in revenge for the murders. Just because of thirteen dead Spaniards, they killed eight hundred Acoma."

"But their deaths did not satisfy Spanish vengeance," he said, pounding his hand with his fist.

"After Oñate set fire to Acoma, he ordered all men twenty-five winters and older to have one foot chopped off, including Joe's ancestor. His wife was sold along with other women to the soldiers, the administrators and the friars to become their whores. Oñate gifted the friars the children under twelve and he tried those over twelve as adults. The Spanish enslaved over five hundred Acoma men, women and children for twenty years."

"After destroying Acoma, Oñate condemned all the innocent pueblos for the rebellion there," he cried out, covering his heart with his hand.

"Shush, everyone is staring."

"Let them stare. It is time they know the truth about the Puebloans."

She rolled her eyes and dragged him by his arm to view a painting of a group of bare-chested Indians on horseback standing on a ridge with spears. The artist painted with an uncanny sensitivity.

"Look. Here's a letter written by the artist, C. M. Russell in 1920: 'I have eaten and smoked in your camp and as our wild brothers would, I call you Friend. Time only changes the outside of things. It scars the rock and snarls the tree but the heart inside is the same. In your youth you loved wild things. Time has taken them and given you much to want. Your body is here in a highly civilized land but your heart lives on the back trails that are grass grown and plowed under. If the cogs of time would slip back seventy winters you wouldn't be long shedding to a breech cloth and moccasins. Instead of being holed up in a manmade valley-you'd be tailing with a band of Navajos headed for the buffalo range. I heap savvy you cause there would be another White Injun among the Blackfeet hunting hump backed cows. My brother, when you come to my lodge the robe will be spread and the pipe lit for you. I have said it.'"

"I never heard of this white man Russell. Had I known of him, I would have invited him into my sweat lodge, offered him a smoke, and asked his help to bring home the bones," he said.

Tears dampened his cheeks and she took his arm. They left the Cowboy Hall of Fame, as silently as they had entered, like two Pecos ghosts.

They drove away from the parking lot.

She tightened her hands on the steering wheel, opening her mouth several times but could not speak to him of her own experience with Oñate.

The miles slipped by.

"I have another surprise for you, Governor, this one more pleasant, I hope," she said veering the truck off I-40 to 7.

At dusk they pulled into an RV area at Hot Springs National Park in Arkansas.

He changed into his undershorts and with skin loose as a turkey neck, settled into the Hot Springs, sighing with delight.

"Ah, this feels like my sweat lodge," he said.

She laughed and splashed him with water.

He splashed her back and they giggled like children.

She literally pushed him out of the springs and worried about the hot water and his blood pressure, not to mention other complications of his age though he claimed to be in better spirits than her.

She readied for bed, climbed in the camper and counted minutes under her breath until he returned from the bathroom.

He climbed into his sleeping bag and they lay back to back, his spine digging into her spine. He may be strong enough to lift himself up to the truck bed, but he felt so frail.

"Good night," she said.

"Pleasant dreams," he mumbled.

She gritted her teeth, yanked the covers to her chin and trembled on the mattress, sneezing at the dust on her nightgown from the night before when the dream catcher hurled her to the Pecos ruins.

Those strangers in her dream made her feel as much an outsider as their invaders were. Even with the approach of their conquerors, she envied those people. A sense of community and family vibrated at their pueblo, making her feel so alone, even with the old man sleeping beside her.

A full moon shone through the camper window, reminding her of a similar moon on a cold windy night last year, January, 1998. After three glasses of red wine, she jumped in the back of one of the trucks that screeched to a stop in front of their house, and she yelled at Steve to go to hell. She only knew one person in the party that roared down the highway headed towards Española. Her old friend from her wild days, Laverne O'Tero, passed her a whiskey bottle. "It's Jack Daniels, only the best," Laverne said.

"Where are we going?" she said, laughing recklessly and thinking, who cares where they are headed so long as it is away from Steve.

"We travel the road of justice. It's the Cuatro Centenario, the Four Hundredth Anniversary of the first Spanish settlement on our lands," Laverne said.

Over the roar of an electric saw wielded by the driver, Laverne hollered into her ear that they had driven to Alcalde, to the new bronze Oñate Monument, to cut off the tyrant's foot in revenge for Acoma Pueblo.

Their victory that night was short-lived because the powers-that-be would soon attach another bronze foot to Oñate's ankle but for one magical evening, when his right foot dropped to the ground with a bang, including a star-shaped spur, they screamed and hollered for joy like a bunch of wild Indians. Like the note they left at the statue that night trumpeted: fair is fair; even if it took four hundred years to enforce justice. Spain convicted Oñate in Mexico City for his crimes against Acoma and expelled him from New Mexico for good but he won his appeal, blaming the unfortunate mess on his nephews and foolish youth, something like that. One of the King Phillips appointed him head of mining inspectors for all of Spain, where he spent the rest of his days wallowing in a bed of Spanish roses.

A feeling of pride now made her eyes water and her dream catcher appeared blurry. Her heart pounded as loud as the booming sound when Oñate's foot had hit the ground. At the same time, sadness filled her that she couldn't tell the old man about her conquest.

"He'd just lecture me about drinking, the old hypocrite. Nor has he ever liked Laverne," she mumbled into her pillow.

She couldn't remember now what she and Steve fought about that night. She had been more selfish than filled with any great passion for the Indian cause though she now tossed and turned in the camper, worrying she was too Native American and not only carried a four-hundred-year-old grudge against Oñate but also against the old man. He had abandoned her to St. Mary's in Santa Fe when she barely reached the sink. Twenty-eight years separated her from that seven-year-old girl yet she still clucked about like a chicken, never accepting who she really was and confused as ever. Many times he pointed out she was like him. He once told her, "You cannot deny what you are. The snake marked you and this gift will allow you to see into the darkness of a man's soul."

Moisture gathered at the corners of her eyes. She only pretended to be tough and trembled with terror at her spinning dream catcher, which hypnotized and paralyzed.

The clock ticked.

Her chest heaved.

The stink of dirty socks invaded her sinuses mixed with Old Spice Aftershave.

Reddish dust blew from her dream catcher's tiny hole until she lay in the midst of a dust storm with granules flying about. Dirt piled like reddish snow drifts around the mattress.

The truck shifted beneath her and the dirt sucked her under like quicksand.

She kicked her arms and legs, struggling to breathe, physically feeling a lack of air like her death was really happening; her waist was locked in a vise, her lungs smashed.

Dust covering her transformed into disturbing images of dead bodies. Corpses trampled her, each slammed back by a booming sound, burying her beneath piles that crushed her. She could see out with one terrified eye between gaps of decaying flesh.

The dust storm settled into waves of shimmering dirt. Darkness behind her eyelids burst into visions of flowers, a field of red and blue roses...then transformed into a field littered with bodies.

The earth threw her upward and expelled her to the center of Pecos Pueblo.

She staggered around the grand plaza, surrounded by sobbing men, women and children. A couple hundred dead or dying Indians lay scattered about the plaza. Wives pummeled their chests with their fists.

Children screamed out, "Father!"

Old men cradled the heads of sons in their laps.

About four hundred Spanish soldiers encircled this scene, pointing smoking harquebuses at the crowd.

The arrogant Spaniard who sat on his decorative horse was made of bronze like his statue in Española. He removed his helmet and wiped his face with a handkerchief. His beard trembled with a deep sigh. He addressed the pompous man mounted beside him.

"Well, Vicente, Pecos is the last of the pueblos to feel your vengeance for your brother's murder. You have done me a service, Nephew. We do not have to worry any more about the pueblos revolting. We have shown them what Spanish vengeance is."

"Fray Francisco," Oñate yelled, standing on his stirrups, and looking over the soldiers' heads.

An old friar hobbled towards him.

"Too bad my nephew's death ruined our first Christmas in Nuevo México," Oñate said.

"Our camp master will be most sorely missed, most Royal Governor, especially by his family. My condolences," Francisco said, bowing his head obediently.

"Yes, I have the sad duty of writing to his mother, my sister. You have my permission to get back to building your church," Oñate said.

"God's work is coming along," Fray Francisco said, pointing to a glob of mud and lumber stacked on a ridge about a thousand feet northeast of Pecos Pueblo, and the skeleton of a rectangular adobe.

"All these heathen souls are not yet ripe for picking but with a little coercion, eh, I believe we will make Spain proud of us," Oñate said. He nodded with his head for his soldiers to mount their horses.

Four hundred strong, they rode from the pueblo, some with headless turkeys bouncing on their saddles.

Fray Francisco walked beside another Franciscan. They stepped over several bodies and walked near Hollow-Woman.

"We have taken food from them before, but it is said that the theft of a turkey sparked the Acomas' anger," Francisco said.

"Truly, I shall never understand these barbarians."

"Perhaps if you bother to learn their language..."

"As you do?"

"I know a smattering but then I am the exception. I know enough to order them back to work on our church without having to use sign language," Francisco said.

Their conversation faded.

The church being constructed was in a different location than the cathedral ruins at Pecos. This initial church appeared much humbler and less ambitious than a cathedral.

A young woman, who looked vaguely familiar, blocked her way and held out a turkey feather.

"See, I managed to save this before they took all our turkeys. The giant bird is sacred to us for its feathers that warm us in winter and adorn our heads at sacred ceremonies where its magical plumes are used as prayer sticks. The savage Spaniards cook this magnificent creature for food. I am a widow now," she said, crumbling to the ground in a sobbing heap, and hugging her turkey feather to her chest.

The woman turned on her back and stared at her with listless eyes. "Why do they blame the rest of us for Acoma? We bowed our heads in obedience to the Spanish and harmed no one. Pray with me, lady," she said.

Hollow-Woman shook her head, no, because she had no faith except for her belief in Grandfather's magic and the Pecos curse. She simply watched the backs of Spanish soldiers march through the gates of the pueblo.

Oñate and his killing machine vanished over the horizon.

A lone rider approached.

He appeared to have ridden his horse hard as it pounded its hoofs against the ground, its big nostrils opening and closing, expelling a foggy cloud that made it seem as if horse and man floated.

A Plains Indian sat upon the horse with slumped shoulders, back bowed, and head leaning forward so that he stared at his lap. His legs dangled from his horse. His head wobbled from east to west. The arch of his arm loosely supported his spear that pointed downward at the ground instead of at his enemies. The wind pushed him and his limp muscles flapped about.

This lone horseman was The-End-of-the-Trail Indian, human-size and come to life.

He and his horse stood out, shockingly white, against the reddish brown Pecos Pueblo, looking as if all their blood had been drained. He appeared ghostlike as he circled the central plaza, his entire being hung in defeat. He seemed oblivious to the carnage around him but when he passed her, he sobbed. His tears were not clear and transparent but red in color and distinct on his white cheeks.

His cries were lost among the crush, as the people tugged the bodies of their dead loved ones.

At first she didn't see the short, old man with grey hair riding behind The-End-of-the-Trail Indian, hugging him around his waist. The old man was missing his feet and he bounced on the saddle. She ran after the horse, yelling, "Grandfather," but he kicked his ankles against the horse—just like him to ignore her.

The dragging of corpses across the earth made a whirling sound and the braids of The-End-of-the-Trail Indian swirled around his head.

She blinked her burning eyes and was transported back to her camper where her dream catcher spun, the feathers flapping in the air like bird wings.

The corpses whirled through the tiny hole in the center of the net.

The-End-of-the-Trail Indian shrunk smaller and smaller as it circled her head. She protected her face with her arms from tiny clods of horse shit. She peeked through the cross of her wrists as The-End-of-the-Trail Indian and Grandfather vanished through the hole. There was a scream and a whinnying, then Grandfather's snores.

She snuggled closer, wrapping her arms around his feeble body, checking to see that his feet were attached at his ankles. He whimpered in his sleep.

7

In Memphis she drove down Elvis Presley Boulevard just to gawk at Graceland.

Grandfather looked exhausted and they need not rush and break their necks to get the bones. It's not like those two thousand or so skeletons could rise and walk away like in her dream.

"Are you alright, Governor? You holding on?" she said.

"A bottle of wine would fortify my blood."

"We may as well gas up now then."

She turned the wheel around, found the closest station and ordered him to, "Wait here."

She walked into the store, purchased a bag of his favorite cookies, a pack of gum and his favorite cheapo wine. She handed him the package then waited at the bathroom for a nun to finish her business.

The nun stepped on her foot when she came out and didn't apologize.

Hollow-Woman stiffened at the nun, held her tongue and limped into the restroom, feeling like a child again at St. Mary's.

She dried her hands on her jeans and lifted her bangs from her forehead to examine her scar in the cracked mirror. She wiggled her eyebrows and her scar folded in and out, like a snake opening and closing its fangs.

Her reflection faded then reappeared into a full-blown scene from childhood. The scene in shadows looked like a negative from an old movie of a seven-year-old girl sitting alone on a bed in a room lined with bunk beds, made up military style. The birthday girl held a needle and thread in one hand and in the other hand, a torn dress. She sucked on her finger because she had pricked herself. She would not cry out. She would not show any weakness. She would not reveal her homesickness. She shut her eyes yet she still saw the other girls' fingers point at her forehead.

"She has a rattlesnake mark. She is a witch," they sang, dancing around her.

She vomited on her bed.

The girls took a step back and screamed, "You threw up snake venom," they recited.

She thrashed about as they accused her of being that poisonous Towa girl from Jemez.

"No, I am Hollow-Woman," she hissed, raising her head like a cobra and glaring at them, pleased they feared the snake girl. She lifted her upper lip and snarled with her eye teeth like fangs. She did not reveal all her secrets and did not correct them that she only lived at Jemez and was really an endangered species from Pecos, the last of her kind, melting, fading...just like the childish scene in the mirror at a gas station in Memphis.

The glass was now in shadows but her reflection bluntly revealed a grown woman with two fang marks stretched on her forehead that would never let her forget she was of the Snake Clan. She pressed against her scar. The girls from her youth lied; she never vomited snake venom from her system; poison still filled her soul. She walked back to the truck, clenching her fists and vowing to become a better person.

She sat on the driver's seat and kissed his forehead.

"I love you, old man," she said.

He merely looked down at the floor and hugged his bottle of wine.

They caught I-55 north to Jackson, Missouri.

He slept most of the way.

She exited off the freeway and wound her way to a street named Moccasin Springs. They pulled up at the Trail of Tears State Park and he asked for her help to climb down from the truck.

One look at Grandfather and they did not ask for proof he was over sixty-five and eligible for a senior discount camping fee.

They feasted on canned beans, roasted wieners and Oreo cookies.

She popped an Elvis CD into her player and put on her earphones. He would not allow her to play music on her truck's CD player while they traveled because he complained how much her music hurt his ears, the old fart. He should talk. His flageolet busted the sound barrier. She had her own theory of why the Pecos Pueblo collapsed. All the musicians gathered one day in the main plaza for a concert. POW! They shattered the adobe, splintered the apartments, and flattened the pueblo with a few notes blown through hollowed bird bones.

She sang silently to the song, *Lady Madonna*, moving her head to the beat. When she got to the lyric, did you think that money was heaven sent, Grandfather nudged her knee.

"Read me more of the thief's diary," he said.

She sighed and put her CD player away, always ready to treat the old man nicer when she felt guilty. She wrapped him in his blanket and balanced his hat on his head. She stroked his cheek.

She crossed her legs, Yoga style, dragged her butt closer to the fire, and thumbed through the diary.

"April 1, 1915.

We have unearthed many relics here, bits of pottery and straw. At first, the trash mounds looked like a natural part of the ridge until we found trash at each level of digging. 'What we have here is a time capsule of these ancients, centuries of discards thrown away in chronological order,' I said. 'The Indians have built upon their trash. No garbage dumps,' I joked. I am examining the changes in pottery and other remains, and I believe I can devise a scheme to interpret the time sequence of the Pecos Pueblo, from beginning to the end of these unfortunates. I should be able to date the relics we unearth by using stratigraphy against the great trash mounds. Perhaps I'll call my system Basketmaker and Pueblo. There is a potential for hundreds of years of fertile garbage here, including carved stone figures and decorated pottery, some intact. I wrote Mother, 'You never thought your son would be a garbage man.'"

"Garbage? Bah! The thief unearthed the sustenance of a people like he dug in their veins to remove their nutrients. Their blood nourished the Pecos earth. Their hearts beat beneath the surface. Their dreams decorated their pottery. Their hunger devoured their eating utensils. Their spirituality embodied their carved stone figures. You cannot categorize a man's soul into Basketmaker and Pueblo. Man is as complex as the path of the great hunter, the tornado. One never knows which way it will gallop and where it will graze," Grandfather said.

"Well, the saying goes, one man's garbage is another man's treasure. Listen to his words as they spill from the prairie dog's pen," she said.

"This evening Jack and I engaged in a lively discussion about how New Mexico makes a good argument for separation of church and state. Under Spanish rule the king either appointed the governor or sold the governorship, in either case, the new governor spent a lot of his own money to outfit an army to travel to the outback that was New Mexico. Being so isolated from Mexico City, New Spain's headquarters, a New Mexico governor's supremacy went unchecked, except by the friars who competed for power.

Our historian came into my tent and got involved in our discussion of church and state. He stated the case of Governor Pedro de Peralta who ruled New Mexico from 1610 to 1614, and his struggle with Fray Isidro Ordóñez. In Peralta's case, Fray Ordóñez constantly undermined him, ultimately resulting in the governor's excommunication and his imprisonment by the Franciscans.

The Indians also involved themselves in Spanish politics, sometimes poisoning a friar who meddled in their affairs.

But to get back to the ruins, the biggest piece we have unearthed so far is part of a wall of the Spanish Mission Catholic Church named Nuestra Senora de Los Angeles de Porcíuncula. The union of the pueblos and the church was forced. The friars ordered the Indians to kneel and kiss their hands and obey them else they would torch their pueblos. They threatened the Indians with Spanish swords or burning them alive if they injured their friars. We have found many smashed idols of stone and wood, many dated around 1620, the time that Fray Ortega, as guardian of the Pecos Convento, vowed to abolish all heathen idolatry and undertook a war against their beliefs. He was the first zealot but would not be the last.

Fray Ortega also engaged in a war of sorts with Juan de Eulate, Royal governor of New Mexico from 1618 to 1625. As my historian pointed out, Church and State warred numerous times before this. From the beginning, both Franciscans and governors competed for its riches, which turned out to be the Indians.

Fray Ortega accused Governor Eulate of being in league with the devil. At every turn, Eulate frustrated the attempts of the friars as they toiled in the vineyard of the Lord, which is what the Franciscans labeled

New Mexico, the red grapes being the Indians, but the governor felt those grapes were his. Eulate did his utmost to prevent the friars from using Indian labor to build their missions. Removing them from their fields to build churches meant the Indians' crops fell short, which cut into Eulate's profits as prime picker.

But Eulate acted as no hero to the natives even though he did allow them their idolatry and freedom to live with their wives and concubines, which caused the friars to label the governor the anti-Christ.

Eulate's other enterprises involved kidnapping Indian children and selling them as slaves to the colonists. Phillip III, himself a religious zealot, considered Eulate's slaving legal so long as the stolen Pueblo children learned their Catholic catechism.

Eulate sent out his own apostles, Indians who mingled about the pueblos exalting their idols and instructing them not to go to mass or obey the friars. He proclaimed the governor the Puebloans' best friend and the friars their mortal enemies.

With the Church under Eulate's iron fist, Fray Ortega had the insane idea to build a cathedral at Pecos, large enough to hold all two thousand or so Pecos souls. Fray Ortega at this time lived in an austere convento of a few rooms adjoining the Pecos ruins to the south."

She closed her eyes, seeing once more the small church being built in her dream then flicked her eyes open to the old man's scrutiny. She cleared her throat and continued reading.

"But as fate would have it, Eulate intervened and stopped all heavenly construction at Pecos. Nor would he allow any repairs of existing churches or conventos at any other pueblos. He even threatened to hang any Indian laborers who refused to stop building.

In retaliation, the friars excommunicated Eulate and vowed to inform against him.

He threatened to whip them with two hundred lashes.

The arrival of wagons bursting with supplies along with peace maker Fray Chavarría, the new custos and head of the Franciscan priests, halted this battle for now. Fray Chavarría transferred Fray Ortega to Taos where the Indians fed him tortillas made with maize, mice meat and urine."

Grandfather laughed and she grinned at him.

She read, "Fray Chavarría replaced Fray Ortega with Fray Juárez, who recommenced building a cathedral at Pecos. Only a miniscule portion of the 300,000 sun-dried mud blocks used to build the church of 1621 remain. I don't know how the Indians managed with each block weighing about forty pounds. We have taken apart one of the blocks and found in the adobe: chips of bone, pottery and charcoal pieces so, the dirt to make the mud for the church walls was probably dug from the pueblo garbage."

Grandfather sounded like he choked on a skull. "When we get back to Pecos and rebury the stolen ones, I will destroy the ruins with my bare hands. So the Catholics even used the people's bones to build their church. Don't you see these are more of our ancestors who cannot join the cloud people in eternal rest? Pecos bones are the bricks and their blood the mortar that holds together the walls of the Spanish cathedral, a church built on fire and death," he said, spitting and wiping his mouth with the back of his hand.

She swallowed some air, sipped a water bottle and continued reading.

"My historian tells me, 'While the men hauled earth and water and the great quantity of wood needed for scaffolding, the actual laying up of walls in Pueblo society was women's work. He quoted Fray Alonso de Benavides who wrote that 'the women poked fun at men building walls so they refused, even under the whip.' Those Pecos women must have been muscular to build the mission with forty-pound bricks.

In its heyday, the massive church resembled a 1500's fortress in the design of a gothic Mexican-adobe cathedral at the end of the world, which made it stand out like an extraordinary sore thumb, at least to the Indians who broke their backs during its construction. The natives also built at this time a new two-story convento with covered patio, walkway and balcony.

The free Indian labor used by both friars and colonists was illegal. The Viceroy in Mexico in charge of New Spain also frowned upon their interference in annual pueblo elections. Nor were they supposed to run their livestock within three leagues of the pueblos.

Along with the supply wagon came orders from the Viceroy in Mexico, both Eulate and the friars were to halt their abuses against the Indians."

"Ah that it was so but Mexico is a long way, especially by horse-back," Grandfather said with a heartfelt sigh.

"Listen to this," she said and peered at the diary.

"My historian tells me that the Spanish government eventually tried Eulate for his crimes and because of him, the Holy Office in 1626 established the Spanish Inquisition in New Mexico. The battle between church and state continued, coming to a head when Governor Lopez in 1660 was accused of being a Jew, along with his friends. The governor died in an Inquisition prison. His accuser, Fray Posado, excommunicated his successor, Governor Peñalosa. The governor then arrested Fray Posado at the Pecos convento, placed guards outside the church and threatened to even kill St. Francis, if the saint came out. He boasted he would hang the pope if he tried to excommunicate him. In the kingdom of New Mexico, Governor Peñalosa claimed to be the prince. In the middle of his term, Peñalosa had left New Mexico to search for Quivira. He had returned, claiming to have found the magical land where golden cups hang from trees. But before he could go back to Quivira to retrieve the riches, the Inquisition arrested the womanizing governor, seized his property, and banished him from New Spain. These were just a few of the governors arrested by the Inquisition.

One upside for the Pecos in building the cathedral was that the friars taught some men the trade of carpentry, and they traveled to other pueblos to build."

"Bah, carpentry attributed to our depopulation. We are based on community and a skill that allows a member to work away from the pueblo is a ticket out. This is what happens nowadays when children leave the family bosom and move to work in Albuquerque. Today, the population of all the pueblos has dwindled by the young ones who wish to live elsewhere," Grandfather said.

"Well, people should have the freedom to choose where they want to live, Governor."

"Read." He poked his finger against the diary.

"A duty of the guardian friar of a pueblo was to feed and clothe the poor. To this end, they forced the Indians to provide cattle and corn."

"Bah. No more lies for tonight; I cannot bear to hear anymore. Franciscan friars enslaved and whipped our people to build their mighty mission with the mud of the Pecos River, their bones and burial pottery," he said.

"I'm sure some of the friars acted like holy men. You mustn't get so riled, Governor."

"The back-breaking labor killed many. Pecos blood flowed from broken skin and intermixed with pine cut from the Sangre de Cristo Mountains when our men carried the heavy logs on their backs and their shoulders as they made their way back down the mountain to build the Spanish church. The Sangre de Cristo Mountains translates into the Blood of Christ Mountains because the Savior's blood runs through the pine trees of our mountains, along with our people's blood due to the cruelty of our conquerors, or pacifiers, as they later called themselves, men of the same brand as Oñate. I am going to bed."

She mumbled good night and sat by the fire listening to a Rolling Stones CD.

After the last song, she took a shower and readied for bed.

She lay quietly beside the old man, listening to him puff air from between his lips. She had been a wild teenager and broke his heart with her use of drugs and alcohol to ease her pain, this hollowness she was born with. She took a deep breath to loosen the tightness in her chest; she left those days behind her. Lord knows, she loathed herself but because of her love for Steve, she cleaned up more than a dozen years ago.

The old man turned on his back and kicked her in his sleep, scratching her leg with a ragged toe nail. She resisted the urge to kick him back. Touché. He broke her heart when he abandoned her at St. Mary's. Funny he should rant about young people leaving the pueblo for the city when he dropped her off at the school and just drove away. She only saw him then at Christmas and summer vacations. He promised so many times to come get her for other holidays and school breaks, but usually wound up drunk and forgot about her. There was that one Thanksgiving he picked her up and drove her to a fast-food diner to eat the longed-for hamburger, which ended up a quarter-sized patty buried in a soggy mess of mustard, pickles and grease.

Her thoughts drifted to her education and the nuns' attempts to Americanize her and the other girls. Annihilate the Indian and save the girl, was their motto. The nuns changed her name from Hollow-Woman to

Holly, which she still called herself when the old man wasn't around. Steve called her Holly as an endearment and because he hated her given name.

It did not take her long to get used to the name Holly because the nuns punished the girls for using their Indian names or if they spoke Towa, Tewa, Tiwa, Keres, Zúni or any other Pueblo, Navajo or Apache languages. However, they kept their silence around the nuns and when alone, spoke in their Native tongues so the girls learned to speak English with a guttural accent.

Every year, a nun chopped off her hair, a sinful vanity the nun claimed. She stripped off her clothes and locked away her heathen clothing for visits home. The nun threw her in a tub and scrubbed her raw then handed her a uniform to wear, with outstretched fingers like she feared contamination.

Hollow-Woman blamed the nuns for her lack of curiosity to know about her ancestors since they beat the Indian out of her with an unholy relish. They preached the Catholic god to her. The nuns sparsely educated the students on Native American history, instead shoving white-man propaganda down their throats in a teaching style the government felt would assimilate the Indian into white culture and chip away at their nativeness.

She twisted on the mattress beside Grandfather and struggled to concentrate on her memories. Tears dotted her eyelids and mucus bubbles wet her nostrils. She shouldn't think about school and her unhappy youth but once again, Sister Catherine's face floated before her, contorted with rage and sweat on her forehead, her glasses jiggling as she yelled. Hollow-Woman couldn't recall now what she did to anger the fat sister; many incidents in the previous five years got her in deep water. Sister Catherine was exceptionally brutal that morning. Sister knew she couldn't hurt her with beatings so she shouted at her, you killed your mother, you wretched girl.

No, Sister Catherine, I never knew my mother.

You killed her at birth; your Grandfather said so the day he enrolled you. He said show patience with your wildness because you have never known a mother's touch. We will overlook your abomination just this once.

She hissed at the nun and held up her fingers like claws.

Sister Catherine took a step back from her with a look of revulsion.

She listened for her fading steps and heard a lot of clinking and clanking of trays. All the other girls gathered at the cafeteria for breakfast.

She pulled her handmade doll from under her pillow. The doll's hair was combed in the squash-blossom style of an Indian maiden with a huge bun rolled on each ear, looking like Star Wars' Princess Leia from a movie magazine. Every twelve-year-old longed to see the movie that just came out, but she had never been to any motion picture show, not even a drive-in movie. She sniffed the doll's real human hair and rubbed the softness against her cheek. For seven weeks her mother labored with love to make this doll, even cutting her own long hair and pasting her locks on the doll's head. Her mother must have had a premonition her baby would be a daughter.

She stuffed the doll in her school knapsack, along with a candy bar, and then wiggled out the dorm window. She balanced her toes on the branch of a tree, reaching her hands to a lower branch. She stretched her monkey arms and danced some fancy footwork across some branches before dropping to the ground, hunkering and scanning the area for any spies.

She hitched a ride to the Hispanic village of Pecos then walked the two miles to the pueblo ruins. It was late morning and the sun strong on her back.

Here, this is where her mother's grave was.

No. There.

Here across from…where? Years of blowing sand had changed the landscape. How forlorn the ruins looked.

The wind blew, fluttering dust around her bone thin ankles, and lifting the hair at the back of her neck because a chanting echoed from a kiva.

Moccasins climbed up the ladder.

Men grunted as their feet stomped against the earth, pockets of red dust whirling around their legs. Their feet spun and feathers twirled around their backs, the eagle and the bear.

She could hear rattling, pounding of drums, and the canary singing of flageolets.

In the midst of these dancing ghosts, a vision walked towards her with hair shorn at the neck, bouncing against her head. A long rainbow-colored skirt whirled around her legs. A piece of her skirt was missing, enough material to make the matching dress of a doll. She had cut the material from her skirt at the exact place of her womb. Blood poured from this hole and the dark-skinned woman paled and grew weaker, staggering towards her, holding her arms out.

She froze, unable to help, not even calling out as she watched her mother die again.

She squeezed her eyes shut and imagined treading water in the womb a dozen years ago, hearing two strong heartbeats. The other heartbeat grew fainter and fainter until she burst from her mother's womb into the light. She had sucked her mother's life from her so that she might live. There was room for only one of them in this world.

A snake hissed behind her.

Grandfather stood on two unbending trees the color of a khaki plant, the fabric quenched with thirst.

"I am always watching you. Do not think that because you are away from me that I cannot see what you are up to," he said.

She threw herself in his arms and sobbed on his stained blue-denim shirt smelling of old wine.

He stroked her hair with a gnarled hand. "Don't grieve so, Child. Your mother knew the risk. Like gambling, one never knows for sure the odds in this harsh life God has given us on the reservation. I could not save her. She died in my arms and my son..."

"What about my father? Tell me about him."

He grunted and looked down at the ground. His shoulders shook and his knees buckled so she grabbed him by his armpits to hold him steady.

She walked him back to his truck and helped him into the passenger seat then she shuffled into the driver's seat. At the age of twelve, she knew how to drive, like most kids on reservations who could ride bareback on prickly horses or steer recklessly behind a steering wheel, along the byways of an isolated pueblo, but this was the first time she ever drove on a highway.

Almost as tall as he, she could reach the pedals if she pointed her toes and leaned way back. She stretched her neck and could barely see above the dash. As champion sixth-grade dodgeballer, other cars were no problem and drivers moved out of her way like judgment day cometh.

All these years later, lying in the camper, she had forgotten he tried to shoulder the blame for her mother's death. She lay listening to his light snoring, trying to recall pleasant memories not tainted by St. Mary's and other times when he treated her kindly.

Her chest grew heavy and she fought the dream catcher's pull but the spinning noise grew louder until she heard the pounding of horses' hoofs.

Dust clouds dirtied her white nightgown buttoned to her neck like a virgin. The baked earth should have scorched her bare feet, but she felt no pain. The fall of boots with star-shaped spurs mesmerized her. Horses unearthed the dirt, causing dust clouds to swirl above the heads of Spanish soldiers clothed in dull armor. The soldiers followed the dust swirling around the robes of eleven Franciscan friars—one short the number of apostles in the New Testament. The monks walked with their heads bowed. They tucked their hands into the arms of robes, blue as the color of the Virgin Mary. Their large wooden rosaries clicked against their knees. The hems of their robes swung around their ankles, making a hissing noise in the dirt as the Franciscans marched.

The friars hovered protectively around a wagon and a thick glass case tied to the center in which a three-foot wooden statue of a lady, bounced and swayed to the left and then to the right. Her wooden eyes stared straight ahead with a look of uneasiness. On the horizon loomed the mud city of Santa Fe.

Hollow-Woman recognized this same wooden statue of the Lady, who in present day Santa Fe resides at St. Frances Cathedral. She witnessed from the shadows a homecoming of the Lady, as the Spanish called the Virgin Mary. This statue is America's oldest Madonna brought to Santa Fe by that same custos and Head Agent of the Spanish Inquisition, Fray Alonso de Benavides, mentioned in the diary as the Franciscan friar from the 1600's obsessed with the idea that all Puebloans were either bloody warriors or witches.

Her dream catcher must have hurled her back to 1625 when the Lady bravely sailed across the great ocean to New Spain to make her home in Santa Fe.

The Lady was carved from Spanish willow and her delicate features painted on the wood. Her clothing appeared wilted from her journey across the ocean. Already, the New Mexico sun parched the bark of her face, cutting wrinkles into her wooden cheeks. A tiny fan in her hands would help cool the Lady during the centuries of dry summer months to come. For now, the Lady was dressed like a Moorish princess with a Castilian mantilla cascading from a Mother-of-Pearl comb protruding from the top of her head. She was clothed in a shimmering golden gown. Ruby earrings sparkled from her wooden ears.

Ah, just what the Spanish need, a feminine touch. Perhaps peace will come now to this land. Maybe the Lady will end the tyranny against the Puebloans and turn the pacifiers into true peacemakers. No more feet cut off at the ankles. No more kidnapping of children. No more enslavement.

The wagon entered Santa Fe and the wheels screeched to a grinding halt before the double doors of an adobe building with the name, Church of the Assumption, carved into the wooden door. Soldiers dismounted and marched ceremoniously, removing the glass case housing the Lady. A friar took a hammer and a nail and pounded a sign beside the name of the church. The sign proclaimed: *Holy Office of the Spanish Inquisition Established 1626, New Mexico.*

Fray Alonso de Benavides brought the terror of the Inquisition to New Mexico, for Indian, colonist, and governor alike.

Two of the friars released the Lady from her imprisonment.

The double doors of the church parted, as if by magic.

Hollow-Woman peeked into the church and sniffed. A smell of musk permeated the adobe and a gray cloud obscured the wooden altar. The friars waved their censors containing incense, around the pictures of Santos painted on wooden slabs that hung from the walls.

The friars gently stood the Lady on a carved-out crevice in the adobe, displaying her in the most prestigious corner.

The Lady looked over the heads of the friars and stared back at her.

She looked into this Lady's eyes before in modern Santa Fe and the Lady did not look so sad then. The friars may have the harshest faces, but the Lady had the most mournful eyes. Her wooden shoulders slumped from the weight of her rich clothing, perhaps because a friar hammered a sign at her feet proclaiming her, La Conquistadora. The all-seeing Lady must know that the Spanish Inquisition would give her, a woman, credit for the witch burnings and hangings to come.

Pity moved her for the Lady, who seemed as much a prisoner of the male-dominated church as she was of the male-dominated Indian reservation.

The friars knelt before La Conquistadora but the Lady ignored the Franciscans. The Lady still stared at her and blood flowed from her eyes.

Hollow-Woman reached out her fingers to the Lady.

The statue seemed to shrink as the double doors to the mission church slammed shut with a bang. The Lady was trapped inside with only the male company of friars.

A rush of wind blew from the slamming of the church doors. The wind swirled dust around the Santa Fe streets, and erected adobe buildings from spinning cones of dirt. Native American men carried logs upon their backs under Spanish whips.

Native American women and children begged on the streets for food.

A cone-shaped shadow of dust encircled her so she wilted in the eye of a puny tornado and coughed.

The wind blew stronger and scattered the shadow of dust which no longer protected her. A ray of sunshine beat down upon her head, singling her out.

"Don't starve the people and enslave them," she yelled, clenching her fists to her sides.

The people turned their weary heads to her and eyed her with fear.

Why didn't any of *them* speak up? They simply gawked at her.

The sun shone brightly, yet she looked out through a haze. Some sort of veil covered her face and entire body, imprisoning her arms to her ribs. Her ankles touched. When she breathed, a gooey substance contracted and expanded in her nose.

Hooded men in blue robes surrounded her.

She wiggled but could not free herself from a veil, a living membrane that covered her body from head to toe.

One friar moved his face closer and blew his foul breath in her face. Deep marks on his cheeks appeared as if he mercilessly whipped his skin with branches. His eye sockets sunk into his head. His cloudy, light grey eyes appeared like a dead man's eyes.

The monk jabbed his finger at her.

Her heart slammed against her ribs.

"This woman who accuses us of starving the heathens is of the Snake Clan. She is a snake disguised as a woman," he said in a booming voice.

The same gooey substance covered her mouth and her only protest sounded like a muffled hiss.

"I, Grand Inquisitor of Santa Fe, sentence you to death by strangulation, Witch."

Two hands snaked from behind and grabbed her.

Through the haze of her membrane she watched skeletal fingers wrap around her neck. The bones of Fray Alonso de Benavides rattled as he shook her neck so that her head rolled around her shoulders.

He spun her and she looked into the hood of his robe.

His skull grinned even as he squeezed her throat.

The skeleton lowered his teeth to her mouth and kissed her.

He seemed amused by her choking noises...then...blessedly...everything went black.

Her dream catcher abruptly stopped spinning and hurled her back to the semi-present.

Bones flew from the center of her dream catcher and a large bone, perhaps the femur, poked against the back of her throat so that she gagged, choked and smothered.

She pulled the femur bone from her throat and sat up on the mattress, gasping for air with her fist shoved between her teeth. Scary, shitty nightmare. Her mouth still tasted like rancid bone. Just thinking about the dream tightened her chest. The nightmare had seemed so real, she coughed to rid herself of the sensation of choking to death.

Beside her, the old man snored.

She kicked him for sending her a nightmare.

He merely turned on his back and grunted, once more blowing puffs of air between his lips.

She rubbed her sore toe; he was bonier than she guessed.

8

Of course Grandfather knew about her dream. While she prepared breakfast, he hovered like a hawk, swinging his burlap sack
in his hand.

He wolfed his food down, and then waited for her to finish eating.
He tapped his tennis shoe and twiddled his thumbs. He shoved his face
in hers as soon as she poked the last mouthful in her mouth.

"The Pecos held another lady in such high esteem they did not
abandon her when they left their home," he said, opening his bag.

He unfolded a piece of burlap and handed her a wooden slab
shaped in an arch that reminded her of the tablets of the Ten Com-
mandments. A carving of the Virgin Mary, in high relief, protruded from
the slab.

"She is the Patrona of the Pecos people, Our Lady of Light who
once hung on the ancient church doors of Pecos," he said.

She gasped at the same high lady of Santa Fe known by many
names, but time ravished this Lady and rubbed her head bald so her
forehead appeared big and smart.

"How ironic, don't you think that the Lady at St. Frances Cathedral once called *La Conquistadora*, is today known as Our Lady of
Peace?" he said.

Before she could answer he walked away to the park bathrooms.

"You're called by so many names," she said to the Patrona. She
outlined the circular head and flicked at each dot that formed a halo.
Her wooden heart sounded hollow yet she prayed, "Lady of Peace,
Lady of the Rosary, Lady of Light."

She scrubbed at the Lady's image but could not make the Lady
sparkle. Like that other lady, La Conquistadora her twin sister, this lady
was fashioned from brittle wood but unpainted, worn, and draped in
poor clothing.

She rewrapped the Lady in burlap and placed her on the truck
floor.

When he returned from the bathroom, they entered the Trail of Tears State Park visitor center. She paid ten bucks to tour the exhibits.

He clung to her hand as they looked at haunted pictures of Cherokees looking out from a concentration camp located near Charleston, Tennessee.

"We are lucky we have always been pueblo dwellers and not nomads hunting after our food," he said.

"Were we, Governor? Listen to this Trail of Tears history."

She opened the pamphlet and read.

"In 1830, President Andrew Jackson passed the Indian Removal Act. The Cherokee Indians had the misfortune to have gold discovered on their Georgia lands. Even though the Supreme Court ruled for the Cherokees, President Jackson took their Constitutional rights away. This Trail of Tears State Park is a memorial to nine of the Cherokee groups, forced to march a thousand miles, most barefooted, to an appointed reservation in Oklahoma. On December 15, 1838, the Cherokees reached this site in Illinois where they spent the rest of the brutal winter."

"1838 is when our people were forced to abandon our pueblo," he said.

She squeezed his arm and continued reading.

"Of the 15,000 Cherokees forced to relocate, 4,000 died, which is why their path from the concentration camps of Tennessee to Oklahoma is called the Trail of Tears or in the Cherokee language, Nunna daul Tsuny."

The old man chewed on his fist and looked down at the floor.

"Ah, there now, Governor, though they lost over a quarter of their population, it says here the Cherokees are today the biggest Native American nation," she said.

"Before the white man came, I have heard there were ten million native sons and daughters of America. It took the white man three hundred years to decrease the Indian population to one million. Regardless of their deaths, whether through diseases the white man brought, bloodshed, or starvation, the whites are to blame."

"Did the 1830 Indian Removal Act force our people to leave Pecos?"

He handed her the royal ceremonial staff and wobbled towards the bathroom, holding out his arms.

A walk to stretch her legs before the long drive seemed like a good idea. She left the visitor's center and maneuvered a concrete pathway, carrying the staff in her arms like a baby. How ironic the Trail of Tears State Park was located in Jackson, Missouri, a town probably named for President Andrew Jackson, a man instrumental in their tragedy.

At a storyboard for the Bushyhead Memorial a painting of a minister dominated the center of the story.

The memorial consisted of a tomb in front of a small brick wall, covered by a canopy. In the background grew a cluster of trees and grass. A brass marker on the concrete tomb read: Here is buried, Princess Otahki, daughter of Chief Jesse Bushyhead, and wife of Sam Hildebrand. One of the several hundred Cherokee Indians who died here in the delayed (by ice) crossing of the Mississippi River in the United States forced exodus from Tennessee, North Carolina and Georgia to the Indian Territory (now Oklahoma) in the severe winter of 1838-1839.

A note attached to the tomb corrected the eulogy. Jesse Bushyhead, a Baptist minister, was actually the brother of Nancy Bushyhead Walker Hildebrand, otherwise known as Princess Otahki.

She leaned against Nancy's tomb, claiming the right to call her Nancy because she, too, was born a princess. She nervously pounded the royal staff against the concrete as if she was really somebody, Princess of all Pecos. Being the last of a species did not give her a rare priceless feeling but the sensation of being hunted. She imagined Nancy once felt hunted when the army rounded up the Cherokees.

Yes, Nancy's spirit was here, restless to tell her story.

A vision flashed before her of Nancy, crossing the Mississippi with her husband.

Nancy sat on the ferry but could still feel the freezing water, though the sun peeked through the clouds and melted shards of ice, causing the river to overflow. Others, who already made the crossing, scampered to higher ground.

Her stomach gnawed her intestines because the day before she ate only a piece of salt pork, half-frozen.

No matter how much her husband Lewis hugged her, the cold would not abate and her breath skated across her icy lungs making her cough.

Her brother Jesse touched her forehead which he complained of being hot—yet her heart chilled at the ice, twelve inches thick, that again floated on the Mississippi, preventing them from crossing.

Barely aware of Lewis and Jesse speaking in low voices, she shivered under both Lewis' blanket and her own. The frigid ground burrowed into her back and the wind howled through the trees, struggling to lift the blanket from her.

Lewis may have held her but she wasn't sure.

Her heart froze solid like an iceberg at thoughts of her children. Where did the soldiers take Sara and Ebenezer? Were her son and daughter even alive? White troops rode to their home near Cleveland, Tennessee and broke down their door. Soldiers threatened them at gunpoint, allowing them precious little time to collect their belongings.

Her pottery shattered with a crash when the soldiers purposefully knocked the butt of their rifles against their household goods, trying to do as much damage as possible. But these were sins of individuals with no respect for Cherokees. Only a monster country would separate a mother from her children.

All she had left of Sara was her favorite doll that she grabbed from the table when the army man grabbed her by her hair because she refused to leave her home. Since then, she hugged Sara's doll close to her heart, consumed with guilt that she angered a soldier so he sent Sara and Ebenezer away to another stockade. The doll offered scant comfort; and a tapping in her chest cracked her heart like a cube of ice.

Goosebumps slid up Hollow-Woman's spine when she recalled Kidder's diary and a part she hated most. His words haunted her: I found an ancient doll and considered sending the doll home to Mother; she is a collector. But, Mother is hygienic so I will ship the doll with other relics back East.

For some freakish reason, this doll found at Pecos upset her more than any skeletons dug up and shipped to Boston.

She placed her hand against her empty womb and pressed her back against Nancy's tomb. She had a doll with human hair connecting her to her own mother. She dreamed nightmares of lying with her mother in her grave, daughter and mother clinging to each other for all eternity in death, the way they could never touch each other in life. The lump in her throat nearly choked her because Kidder expressed his sympathy for a double find, a woman skeleton holding an infant skeleton in the crook of her arm: Sadly, I have found a mother and child who perished together, so he wrote.

Then contrarily, he bragged about his discovery, 'a rare find' he labeled it.

What did the mother feel when she held her dying child? Perhaps the child suckled weakly at her breast while it lay there dying, or maybe the mother wasted away from a broken heart since her baby died. Conceivably, all the life sucked out of the baby because it killed its mother at birth.

Kidder must have lifted the bones from their graves and pulled apart mother and child since he made separate piles of adult skeletons and children skeletons. The fragile baby skeleton turned to dust soon as he ripped the baby from its mother's arms. The mother lay there, her eye sockets sunken, her shoulder bones slumped, her arms empty, her mouth open in a silent scream.

During the holocaust, Nazis placed parents on one train and children on another train, to transport them to concentration camps where certain death awaited them.

She closed her eyes and imagined a dead mother and baby. Flesh melted from the woman and child, and they looked like zombies. Their bodies decayed until they turned to skeletons and broke apart. Mother and daughter separated, both screaming. The girl's bony hands reached out to her mother's bony wrists.

Once more, laughter of children filled the air, like in her first dream which had hurled her back to Pecos Pueblo. Such unbearable longing filled her, she groaned and doubled over.

Their laughter turned to cries of Cherokee children dying from hunger, crying from thirst, screaming from soldiers' blows upon their little bodies, moaning from disease, longing for toys they left behind.

Sobs shook beneath this earth. They cried out, "Mommy, Daddy, where are you?"

Baby, I'm here. Nancy lay in her tomb like that skeleton mother at Pecos, her eye sockets sunken, her shoulder bones slumped, her arms empty, and her mouth open in a silent scream.

She wrapped her arms around Nancy's tomb, as best she could, and hugged the cold slab.

"I'm sorry, so sorry. I hope your children lived."

"I'm sorry, so sorry..."

Over and over apology flowed from her lips until strong hands gripped her arms and pried her away from the tomb.

Grandfather picked up the ceremonial staff and led her away from the Bushyhead Memorial.

He stroked her hair with a petrified hand.

"Don't grieve so, Child. One would think she was your mother."

9

They drove north on I-55. He snored lightly, his chin resting on his chest. He always slept this way but never complained about an aching neck, so he must have rubber bands for ligaments. His head traversed a circular route when he napped, stopping every 90 degrees while he blared out snores like a trumpet.

They stopped for lunch in St. Louis and munched on hamburgers and fries, followed by apple pie.

"You look tired," she said.

"It is time for my lunch nap," he said, stretching and yawning.

He opened the camper shell so he could lie down. He grunted, rolled on his side and hugged the royal staff in his arms.

She caught I-70 east and drove with the radio on.

When they stopped for gas in Springfield, he bought a bag of suckers and sat beside her in the truck licking and sucking on the candy.

She cracked, blew and popped her gum, playing bass to his tongue violin. Between them they played a gum pack of symphony movements all the way to Columbus.

She pulled into an RV park at dusk, helped him down from his seat and handed him his staff.

"The ground is uneven and there are rocks around," she warned, holding onto his arm.

He used his staff while they walked to the bathrooms. It seemed as if they were deep in the woods with moss clinging to large rocks and ferns growing about.

The area was peaceful, save for a fox that spied on them from the woods.

He seemed more refreshed after dinner.

He made a round trip to the bathroom then threw the diary at her.

"Read," he said and rolled a cigarette, closing his eyes as he puffed, sighing with contentment.

"June 1, 1915.

I am having trouble sleeping. I close my eyes and dream of sifting through trash looking for buried treasure. My tent has a rotten tomato stench though I have not had a salad in a fortnight. I am awaiting oranges from Stanford University. I placed a bet with my old roommate, Dr. Jonesboro, that I would make an amazing find here in New Mexico dust. He laughed at me. Ha. Jonesboro owes me a crate of fresh oranges. My dig marks the coming of age of American Archaeology! We have found our greatest treasure, the Pecos Indians themselves."

"Bah. They found treasure. They searched for ivory but found only bones. The white men did indeed return to Pecos to find buried beneath the earth a ghost pueblo. Still, their greed was the size of the plains, and they dug and dug to steal the pottery and baskets. They were not content with straw and clay. They lifted our people from their graves and desecrated our land," Grandfather said. He motioned with his hand to continue.

"With today's rubbish pile, we found some skeletons," she read.

"Rubbish? He dares call our people rubbish?" he said, spitting and flicking his cigarette away.

"Well, earlier he said he sifted through centuries of trash piles. That's what an archaeologist does. Calm down and listen to what's next."

"At this solemn moment I ordered everyone to remove his hat while we said a prayer for these poor souls. A smallpox epidemic, the result of European invasion, raged across this land from 1519 to 1524 like the Black Death in Europe and killed half the native population. I wondered if any of these Pecos Indians died of smallpox.

Ha. I stared into the empty eye sockets of one fellow and asked him to tell me his name, but he just lay there with his bones spread across the ground. The skull grinned at me with big teeth, and I somehow felt the poor fellow laughed at me. I knocked on his empty skull and asked him what secrets his bones held but he remained closed-lipped. I drove into Santa Fe to see if anyone there knows the Towa language. I just wanted to hear what these people may have sounded like."

"He thinks we are a stupid people, with empty heads, like white men before him thought. Just because *he* cannot speak to *us* in *our* language, he thinks we are dumb," Grandfather said, clenching his fists until his knuckles turned white.

"Do you want me to stop reading?"

"Go on."

"Someone pointed out an old Indian sitting at the plaza selling blankets. He could say but one word in English—no. I asked a boy, his grandson, if his grandfather could speak Towa for me. The boy said they were from the Nambe Pueblo and spoke Tewa. He suggested I travel to the Jemez Pueblo to hear the Towa language. Perhaps another day since Jemez is about eighty miles. On the way back to the ruins, I debated what to do with the skeletons. I am a Christian man and the thought of desecrating the graves of these poor souls disturbs me, yet I am a man of science, and this is a find of the greatest magnitude. What Harvard might gain from study of these indigenous ancients, both in prestige and future grants, outweighs my conscience."

"Wait. What is indigenous?" Grandfather said.

"It means of the earth from where one is found."

He nodded his head, satisfied.

She continued reading.

"I shall request the university order acid-free boxes to pack the bones for shipment and storage.

I posed for some photographs. Well done."

"Stop, I cannot hear any more," Grandfather said, squeezing his eyes.

"I don't understand why you have me read to you, if it only upsets you. I must warn you that from this date his papers take on a more morbid tone because he became obsessed with the remains of human bones. Over the next several months, he unearthed warriors, women, children, tiny skeletons."

He raised his eyebrow at her.

Aha. The sly fox complained just to gauge her reaction.

"This is like a history lesson, informative but dull," she said, stuffing the diary back in the case and shifting her eyes, anywhere but at his haggard face and his eyes…she disappointed him again. "You have always taught me to speak the truth, Governor."

"Do you know why you are called Hollow-Woman?"

"To torment me?"

"Because you are empty and I do not see the fullness of life in you, Child. When you learn to live, when you learn to love unselfishly, when you learn to not want so much, then you will no longer be Hollow-Woman."

"Grandfather…" but he had silently left her, in his Shaman manner that could make him appear invisible.

She sat until her leg cramped.

She limped to the restroom, washed her face and by the time the bathroom door swung behind her, the cramp loosened. She shook her leg as she walked back to the camper, squinting at the moonless night.

It seemed sunlight shone on the roof and windows and illuminated her dream catcher spinning above like a kaleidoscope. Flashing psychedelic colors made her feel like she tripped out on acid.

Her bare feet no longer tingled like ice but felt scorched from the sun on a rough dirt road.

Beside her shuffled an Indian woman like one of those Chinese ladies whose feet got broken and bound as a child. Dark circles shadowed her eyes and she was dressed like the ancients.

"What year is this?" Hollow-Woman said in Towa.

"It is the year of the Spanish Lord, 1638. My name is Lupe," she said, bowing her head respectfully.

Hollow-Woman introduced herself and offered to share some of the burden of the blankets she carried on her back like a burro.

"I am young in years but hard work has molded my body into an old woman," Lupe said, shrugging her shoulders like the load was nothing. Her back was bent and swollen. Her hands hung nearly to her knees. Her hair was prematurely grey and the lines of her face mapped her despair.

There was a resemblance between her and the old woman. It was like looking into a mirror thirty years from now. Hollow-woman stumbled on the dirt road and bit her cheek which, God almighty stung like a bumble bee.

"There is my home," Lupe said, and pointed to the Pecos Pueblo that rose from the plains, a mile to the west, like rectangular mountain tops of sun-baked mud with windows here and there and brown faces staring out like dots.

"Don Francisco stole much of our land and the water that runs nearby. Ah, I can see by your unbroken body that you are new to the pueblos. Our Royal Governor Luis de Rosas appointed Don Francisco as Encomendero of Pecos, so he is the boss we work for since the Spanish crown claims we are their vassals, and we must pay tribute to our Encomendero. We are the richest encomíenda," Lupe said, lifting her chin proudly.

"I still don't understand," Hollow-Woman said.

"For three successive lifetimes Don Francisco and his heirs collect our tributes as his personal income tax but greed eats at that fat man so he is not satisfied with the corn and the animal skins we bring him. He forced us to the upper lands where the soil isn't fertile and built a great hacienda. In exchange for our land, he gave us sheep. A few days later, he sent his men like thieves in the night and stole our sheep from us. Don Francisco snatched my husband from our fields so he could plant and harvest for him. Jose works their fields and has little time for our own land. Then, Jose must give Don Francisco half our corn crop to pay the taxes. Is it any wonder we starve while the Spanish grow fat?" Lupe said, spitting in the dirt but lacking saliva so all she managed was a hacking cough. "My mouth is so dry because of the drought that has lasted these many years."

"Can you not appeal to the Viceroy in Mexico?" Hollow-Woman said.

"Bah, the Viceroy informed the Spanish here that an encomíenda does not include free labor, but these are empty words from a land far away. Along with summer, we look forward to the Taos Trade Fair to enrich us but this year the fair promises no relief from our hunger, no comfort from peyote buttons the Apaches trade for our goods, nor cotton for our clothing. This past spring, Jose came home from the trade fair with empty pockets. He traded all our goods but had to pay four times as much for the trade because that is the way the Spanish operated the fair, cheating so they can grow richer. Both Puebloans and plains Indians must pay the Spanish with one type of currency but are paid by the Spanish with another type of currency which is worth only a fourth. So, Jose came home poorer while the Spanish went home richer. We should boycott the trade fair but everyone fears what the Spanish will do. Instead of just kicking in our doors to beat us for not appearing penitent in church, they will make arrests and our men will vanish like before," Lupe said.

A wagon pulled in front at a fork in the road and they both jumped back.

The statue of La Conquistadora, also known as the Virgin Mary, also called the Lady, bounced in the bed of the wagon and looked out from her glass travel case with a bored expression in her painted eyes.

Franciscan friars marched beside the wagon, dust swirling around their blue robes, wooden rosaries clicking against their thighs. Each monk held a fiery torch above his head and chanted an eerie Spanish tune, an alabado, a hymn sung at funerals. Fray Alonso de Benavides, Agent of the Holy Inquisition, led their singing.

Hollow-Woman and Lupe fell back a step because of the heat from the torches.

"Perhaps these Franciscans are escorting the Lady to a witch burning," Lupe whispered.

The wagon hit a pothole, not unusual on a dirt road that rains sculpted. The Lady's wooden head smashed against the top of the glass case causing a crack in the glass.

The wagon bounced along until a wheel got stuck in a bigger pothole causing it to stop lopsided on the road.

"Now's our chance," Lupe said, grabbing her hand and pulling her towards the wagon.

With a screeching noise, the glass case slid to a corner of the wagon, causing the Lady to flatten her nose against the glass.

Lupe pushed her face at the Lady and they stood nose-to-nose with the glass between them. Lupe's fingers, thick with calluses, clawed at the glass.

"I have prayed for you, Lady, to come to Nuevo México and see for yourself how your people suffer. Look how my hands have toiled to pay their encomíenda tax with blankets. The flesh falls from my hands to keep the Spanish warm," Lupe said, pressing her blistered, raw palms against the glass.

The Lady seemed to ignore her and stared straight ahead even though Lupe screamed and banged at the glass with her fists.

"Even our children go hungry and die because we must pay our food taxes to the Spanish. The fools outlawed our rain-making ceremonies and so the land remains dry. Bah. They eat our food but do not protect us from the Apaches. Our gods punish us for worshipping the God of the Spanish. This is why the land is so dry. And you...we gave up our gods for you, who do nothing to help us, Lady." Lupe's eyes reflected loss, and a tear fell from her eye as she fell to her knees, begging. "They barged into my house in the middle of the night and took my little girls as slaves and sent them across the great waters to Spain. I'll never see my girls again."

Hollow-Woman knew the sorrow of losing an unborn baby, how much more painful to lose a living child. Even though they stared straight into her eyes, the Lady seemed to avoid their eyes.

"You keep poor company, Lady," Hollow-Woman said, pointing her finger at the agents of the Inquisition who pushed the back of the wagon, trying to remove the wheel from the pothole.

"Do not leave your work to men. The friars do not see our suffering," Lupe said, jabbing a finger at the glass and hissing.

One monk looked right through Lupe as he worked at the broken wheel, but he cocked the hood of his robe in their direction, and so she lowered her head to whisper in the Lady's wooden ear.

"The monks do hear our complaints though and whip us for them. I must warn you, Lady, my words will pain you. Friar MartÃnez raped my niece and slit her throat. He buried her in his convent cell at Los Taos," Lupe said, crossing her chest in the Catholic way. "Everyone at Taos Pueblo knows of this but is afraid to speak against the friar. Beware of the Franciscans who claim to be celibate. I would hide that ring if I was you; even you are not safe from their greed. Keep your eyes open; you have performed miracles, my Lady, so the Inquisition may arrest you for being a witch."

Lupe covered her head with a scarf and motioned Hollow-Woman to follow as she shuffled away, carrying her load of blankets. The weight of her sorrows humped her back.

"Look out," Hollow-Woman yelled at Lupe but was too late.

A wagon went barreling by and hit her.

Lupe lay beneath the heavy wheel, screaming.

A Spaniard sat atop the wagon and whipped Lupe to try to get her to move so the wheel in her gut would become unstuck.

"My Lady," Lupe screamed, lifting her arms to the statue of the Virgin Mary, "Save me."

The friar, who fixed the wheel, rose from his knees and his hood slid from his head. His skull shone in the sunlight and malevolence lined his facial bones as darkness swirled in his empty eye sockets. He lifted a skeletal hand to the Lady's cage and scraped his bony fingers down the glass.

"Ugh." Hollow-Woman gasped for breath, now lying on the mattress. The camper was dirty white in color and no longer psychedelic. Her dream catcher hung motionless from the ceiling.

She hugged with shivering arms the wooden slab, the Patrona of Pecos, the Lady who represented the Virgin Mary, so important to the survivors; they would rather starve than leave her behind at the crumbling pueblo. She wished for even a spark of Lupe's faith. Even though Lupe lay beneath a wagon wheel, she had cried to the Lady to save her. Even though her daughters were shipped across an ocean to work as slaves in Spanish households, her faith remained. How many other children did the Spanish kidnap? What a terrible ordeal for Indian children, enslaved as household servants in Spain, to inhabit a culture so different than their own. At least, children enslaved in the New Mexico colony lived closer to home and perhaps their parents could glimpse them occasionally.

"Save me, Lady," she mumbled to the block of wood but could not muster any passion in her voice, nor conviction, nor hope. Her words fell flat, the affliction of a woman who didn't really believe...in anything.

Her hand relaxed and slid across the slab of wood, and a splinter lodged at the base of her thumb. The splinter stung sharply but she was helpless to remove it, because her dream catcher spun rapidly, hypnotizing her. The direction of the breeze on her face blew counter-clockwise. The breeze did not cool her.

Instead of her nightgown, rich clothing spun from gold draped across her body. A silver lace mantilla flowed to her feet. An enormous gold necklace hung from her neck and weighed down her chest. Her heart sounded like a woodpecker knocking against a tree. She couldn't move her eyebrows and her mouth splintered when she tried to smile.

She stood in the center of this grand mud-baked plaza before, in the old part of Santa Fe where little has changed in hundreds of years. Old Santa Fe, in modern times, still has the look of a Spanish colonial town situated 7,000 feet high near a stream that flows from the Sangre de Cristo Mountains and spills into the Río Grande.

She cuffed a hand to her brow to block out the sun, and peered at the dusty road, but there was only dirt where New Santa Fe should have been. In old Santa Fe, the Palace of the Governors dwarfed all the other buildings. The palace was a low rectangular one-story adobe building, an entire block long, with a carved open porch supported by wooden posts. The porch bordered the entire building.

She recently toured the Palace of the Governors, the oldest con-tinuously occupied building in the United States, in modern day a state history museum. Oñate originally planned the Palace of the Governors and his successor, Peralta, completed the building. The sign hanging in front of the building now differed in that it was not in English, like modern times, but in Spanish. The words proclaimed: El Palaio de el Gobernadoros, establecido 1610 por orden de Nuevo España, which translates to: The Palace of the Governors established 1610 by order of New Spain.

The sign listed names of various Spanish colonial offices housed at the Palace, beginning with the most important office, that of Gover-nor Luis de Rosas, appointed governor of New Mexico, 1637.

Still dressed like a Spanish noble woman, she didn't want to draw attention to her dark Indian skin because she feared being accused of theft. She tugged at the necklace to draw it around her head, but the necklace was short and the clasp stuck so it would not open. The emerald and ruby rings on her fingers were too tight to come off. She tucked her hands under her arms and walked with her head bowed. Dust soon covered her rich clothing and silk robe.

No one seemed to notice her along the porch anyway. Spanish soldiers and government officials lingered with their noses in the air. Other men slapped important-looking papers in their hands and marched into offices. Others marched out of offices, some with a smile on their faces, many with a frown.

In the middle of the street a Spanish soldier whirled his arm above his head and whipped several Indians who had their heads bowed low. One of the Indians, a woman, cried out in pain and held a hand to her bleeding cheek.

Due to her long robe, Hollow-Woman stumbled, regained her balance and didn't actually fall though her clumsiness drew the attention of a soldier. He stopped whipping the Indians, stepped in front of her, and smacked her across the face with the back of his hand. He cussed at her in Spanish. Even given her rich Spanish clothing, an Indian had no right to walk across the porch of the Palace of the Governors. In present day, Native Americans sit on the porch with their legs crossed, selling their jewelry on homespun blankets as colorful as rainbows. What was the punishment in ancient times for an Indian who dared set foot on the porch of the Palace of the Governors to seek refuge from the hot sun?

The soldier stood with one fist raised above his head. He blinked his eyes at the necklace entangled in her long hair.

A carriage arrived and saved her from a beating and questioning. Dust blew about the wheels, creating quite a stir.

The officer spun away from her, snapped his heels, and saluted the black carriage with a fancy-looking emblem painted on the side of the door.

She breathed a sigh of relief because the arrival of the carriage spared her an explanation of why she masqueraded as a Spanish lady.

The carriage ground to a halt; the officer opened the door, bowed and helped down a small, well-fed man who teetered on high-heeled boots.

The fat man wiped the sweat from his brow with an embroidered handkerchief. He looked up to the lean officer with a wolfish face and moustache. "You have news for me, Capítan Gutierrez?" he said.

"We carried out the slave raid as ordered. We killed around seventy Apaches but captured twenty-five. They are able-bodied and can replace the sixteen Puebloans who died in your sweatshops last week. The extra nine you can sell for a hefty profit at Nueva Vizcaya."

"I have also brought prisoners with me from the Pecos Pueblo. Chavez and his men are escorting the slaves. The Pecos claim the Apache refuse to trade buffalo hides and meat for the knives we gave them to trade for us. They returned empty-handed so now, I'll have to work the hide off the prisoners in exchange for my loss."

"Who can blame the Apaches for not wanting to trade food? With a drought that's lasted five years?" Capítan Gutierrez said.

"We must demand even more tribute from the Puebloans then."

"Uh, Governor," he said, wiping the sweat from his brow and shaking in his boots. "Fray Domingo de Espíritu ex-communicated the guards you appointed to watch over the prison cell of Fray Antonio Jiménez."

"How dare Fray Espíritu interfere in my business! Fray Jiménez disrupted my trade profits at Pecos."

"But Fray Jiménez is more than sixty years old. It seems cruel to imprison him."

"Don't go soft on me," de Rosas said, narrowing his eyes.

"This appointment is an affront against you to undermine your governing," Capítan Gutierrez said, snapping his heels together.

"I understand the Inquisition blames me for the death of Fray Miranda at Taos. I did not tell the Indians to murder their missionary, only to disobey him. The friars are such hypocrites. They run their conventos like a general store and the Indians as if they are cattle. I do not work children in my sweatshops as they do; the children turn a better profit when sold to Spain and are treated more humanely as household slaves. I will deal with the custos, Fray Espíritu, myself. He holds another grudge against me because I have recently shutdown one of these sweatshops run by the friars. Come, my friend, join me in a glass of wine. At this rate, our ribs will be sticking out of our chests like the Indians," De Rosas said, slapping him on the back.

The fat little governor strutted into the palace, followed by the swarthy captain.

At her feet, an Indian lay on the dirt. He appeared starving. His chest rattled as he struggled for every breath.

She also labored to breathe due to her heavy rich clothing. Fog blew from between her lips and the air grew cold.

She held her hands to her face, expecting to see her fingers dripping with rubies and emeralds but instead, her wedding ring flashed at her. Like Cinderella, her rich gown was transformed back into her raggedy nightgown. Above her, the dream catcher twirled slowly as though winking at her.

She ran her hands down the front of her bathrobe which resembled an old-fashioned rug that made her want to curl up, like a cat, in front of a roaring fire. The robe held up to the test of time because the best seamstress in the world, Old-Woman, the only female of any influence in her life, sewed it. She had treated Old-Woman so poorly, not realizing until her death how much she loved her wrinkles, and the smell of her oven-baked skin powdered with rising breasts of yeast and gobs of butter for moisturizer. Old-Woman was her first regret. She should have treated her like a grandmother instead of snarling at her and showing her claws like a feral kitten. Even in old age, bent with a hump on her back, Old-Woman had slaved over her as though Hollow-Woman was her own flesh and blood. She had tried her best to be the peacemaker between Hollow-Woman and Grandfather. Her eyes had been weak with cataracts when she had sewed her final gift by hand, her arthritic fingers working the needle though it pained her. Even after all these years the robe she made for her still smelled like fried bread and honey.

Since Old-Woman lived with Grandfather from the time Hollow-Woman was six until her death, she was sort of a step-grandmother and passed away when Hollow-Woman was fourteen. Only then did the role she played in her life hit her like bags of month-old bread. Her heart of stone had shattered at her death and she had run screaming behind her coffin, begging Old-Woman not to leave her all alone with Grandfather. To come back and be her mother. She promised to be like her, kind, patient and forgiving.

For weeks she had sat, paralyzed, unable to believe that Old-Woman was gone. Every day she visited her grave until the weeds grew so tall, she could no longer find her and the piercing wound in her heart shrunk to a tumbleweed prick at the memory of Old-Woman.

She now stroked the robe against her cheek and felt wrinkled hands cup her cheeks; kind eyes stare down at her and a gentle smile brighten her day. No matter how much abuse she hurled at her, all Old-Woman ever returned was a smile and a twinkle from her eye.

Hollow-Woman dug her fingernail into a splinter that lodged from the wooden slab of the Patrona to the base of her thumb. She could not extract the splinter from beneath her skin, which proved she was made from wood after all because of her cruelty to Old-Woman. Youth is so wasted on the foolish. Contrarily, she was not made from wood because wood must contract and expand with the seasons of life whereas she was always stubborn and unbendable.

10

Now that they were only about six hours from Washington D.C., he woke her at five in the morning and paced in circles, anxious to leave Columbus. He promised to rest and spent most of the drive with his eyes closed. He snored lightly a good majority of the trip but still looked exhausted when they drove into the nation's capital.

They stopped for lunch, which did wonders for both their dispositions.

They cleaned up in the bathrooms and he changed into a crisply starched, wrinkled shirt.

The pickup started with a slight spark from the ignition, which worried her. A friend of Steve's checked the truck out thoroughly before their trip and it had passed with flying colors.

She parked at the NAGPRA offices located at the National Park Service on Eye Street so, it felt like big brother spied on them as her truck sputtered and coughed, then ground to a halt.

They walked into the NAGPRA offices.

Let them all stare as if she and Grandfather just stepped off a boat from the muddy Río Grande.

Her ragged tennis shoes flapped against the floor like a bag lady, with dusty briefcase with faded cactus print banging against her torn-jean knee.

Grandfather pounded his blackened ceremonial staff as if he was somebody, the Pecos ghost pueblo governor, sovereign with no subjects save skeletons and his smashed crown a magical hat with broken feather. All decked out in rainbow colored shirt, adorned with squash blossom necklace, his arthritic fingers dripping with turquoise. He hugged Alfred V. Kidder's diary with a pleading look on his face, appearing as if he might fall down on his rickety knees and beg for the bones. Gone was the pride of a Kachina priest who ruled the sun. His eyes bugged out from a haggard, blood-drained face. His belt was wrapped one and a half times around the waist of his stained khaki pants that had the remnants of runny eggs. Any minute now, he might poop his pants.

She hid behind dark glasses, embarrassed because he had looped his burlap sack around his narrow belt, fearing someone might break into their camper and steal the dream catcher. The burlap sack dragged against the floor, sifting the dust of the Pecos ruins with NAGPRA dirt and coming up with dust balls.

After waiting for an hour while she held Grandfather up by his arms, she rocked in a stiff Yankee chair while the woman at a desk eyed them with anxiety, shuffling papers, clicking her pen, avoiding eye contact. The woman must have heard about mal ojo—the evil eye.

Hollow-Woman hummed a nonsensical tune Grandfather taught her when needing to ward off the evil spirits. The tune worked as a child growing up at Jemez, but her stomach churned as the woman overlooked their paperwork. The poison was strong today and she gritted her teeth at the rude woman who questioned their documents, including the ones mailed them by NAGPRA. The woman gawked at them, as if they were the first Native Americans she ever saw with flesh on their bones; apparently, NAGPRA did not get many claimants in person.

Hollow-Woman lifted her head and her hair, like black curtains, parted to reveal her piercing chocolate-brown eyes. Once more she explained their purpose, and long trip.

"Look at my grandfather, how old and tired he is. He has waited nearly a century to reunite with his bones, miss."

"His bones?" the woman said, laughing nervously.

Grandfather looked right through the woman, obviously having taken a dislike to her the minute they sat down. It seemed he thought her even more clueless than she about ancestral bonds.

Hollow-Woman dug her fingernails into the wooden arms of the chair to keep from jumping up and slithering across the desk. This white-starched woman appeared afraid of them. There was a sign which stated that NAGPRA was under the jurisdiction of the Secretary of the Interior, namely Fish and Wildlife and Parks. She hugged her stomach, which trembled with laughter, because they had classified Native American bones as wildlife.

"The bones are my family," Grandfather croaked and Hollow-Woman knew what it cost him as he begged with his eyes for the woman to help him.

Finally, all was in order; NAGPRA approved their grant but they would have to wait until tomorrow to pick up the paperwork which required signatures, since it was so late in the day.

Smiling with few teeth in his mouth, Grandfather shook hands with the woman and her boss.

He let out a deep satisfying breath when they exited the building.

She placed her arm through his and kissed his cheek.

"Let's go visit Popé," she said.

"The famous witch from San Juan Pueblo, Popé, died centuries ago," he said, giving her an astonished look.

"Ah, but he is here, Governor, in our nation's capital for all to admire."

11

He was clearly puzzled as they drove to the Capitol building. It was four in the afternoon and their shoes sounded hollow as they toured the National Statuary Hall and a semicircular room draped in hot pink and red with gold braid. Here, statues of notable persons lined the hall. Each state was allowed two statues, for a total of one hundred. Representing New Mexico, a statue of Popé stood amongst the likes of the founding fathers of the United States, the heroes of the American Revolution, and other larger-than-life figures. His statue was seven-feet tall and carved from pink Tennessee marble, making his statue the only colorful one in the collection.

The text identifying his statue stated that his name was pronounced Pó-pay, which means Ripe Squash. The words described his famous public whipping in the year 1675, after the Spanish Inquisition arrested him for witchcraft. After the 1680 Indian Pueblo Revolt, he became leader of all the pueblos until his death in 1692. Without Popé to plan and lead the rebellion, the pueblo peoples' culture would have been snuffed out by the Inquisition that held colonial New Mexico in an iron grip of religious fanaticism.

His statue was so realistic, whipping scars carved on his back dug into the marble.

Grandfather touched his statue with wonder, rubbing the deer hide blanket draped around one shoulder and patting the ankle-length moccasins.

"Like Moses, Popé is our deliverer," he said.

"The Pueblo Revolt is what the American Revolution was to the American Colonists. He is our George Washington," she said.

"I admire his courage and his passion, which moved him to build an army to defeat the Spanish. Even the Spanish always referred to him as El Popé with great respect, even when they whipped him and especially when they ran from him across the Río Grande. He saved our rituals and way of life. In those days there were not nineteen pueblos like today. The Puebloans lived in seventy multi-storied adobe towns. There were nine basic languages and many could not speak the same tongue. The pueblos were located some distance from each other, scattered about New Mexico like chiseled ant hills.

"How did he bring the pueblos together to attack on the same day?" she said.

"He did it with this," he said, patting a knotted rope Popé held in his hands.

The statue of Popé had a wide-eyed look like even he was astonished he managed to drive the Spanish from New Mexico. It was no surprise that in all her years at boarding school the Indian Pueblo Revolt was never mentioned by the nuns, who were Spanish or white.

"He was the most masterful witch who ever lived and smart as the whip the Spaniards laid upon his back. The pueblos have always used their kivas for council, and he summoned in his Taos kiva three supernatural beings, Kachinas, whom he communed with for five years patiently planning the rebellion, the most successful Indian revolt in history. The fact that Popé could get all the pueblos to revolt against their Spanish subjugators on the same day was pure magic. Do you know where the ogre Kachina, Yowi, got his nickname from?" he said.

She recalled the doll-size wooden Kachina Grandfather gave her for her eighth birthday. Forget Barbie dolls, she had doll-like creatures of Pueblo gods. Over the years she collected a large number of wood-carved Kachinas standing on little wooden circles in her living room, each twelve or fourteen inches tall, each appropriately posed, each colorfully painted, each with accessories like her first Kachina, Yowi, who held a bloody knife in one hand and in the other hand a severed head.

"Yowi is the priest killer," Grandfather had explained when he handed her the Kachina.

Yowi had slipped from her fingers and the wooden head Yowi held broke from his hand and rolled across the floor.

"I remember as a child I broke the Kachina Yowi, and you said he would punish me for my carelessness. Yowi's alligator face has terrified me ever since," she said.

"Indeed, you should be scared because Yowi is Punisher Kachina. He beheaded Catholic priests during the Pueblo Revolt. I believe he was one of the Kachinas in the kiva summoned by Popé to help win the war against the Spanish. From the Shipapu of the kivas, the doorway to the gods, Popé summoned Kachinas from their sacred waters beneath the earth so that all across New Mexico, friars were beheaded and torched. Their missions burned. All that remained of the second church built at Pecos was ashes."

The archaeologist's diary had an entry for July where he wrote about discovering a hidden kiva. He said: Perhaps the kiva was dug in the twelve years between 1680, when the Indians drove out the Spanish and 1692, when the Spanish returned to rebuild a new church atop the old church. The second possibility is the Spanish dug the hidden kiva, and the friars built their church above on purpose, as a symbol of their religion's superiority over that of the Indians, in much the same way the priests earlier subjugated the Puebloans and enslaved them to build their churches. It was growing dark when we made our discovery and I don't know yet how safe the kiva is to enter. Tomorrow we shall see. There is a chill in the air and it feels like fall. I've asked my servant for another wooly blanket.

"Look, the artist of Popé's statue is from Jemez," she said.

"That should make you proud since you claim to be Jemez and not Pecos."

She placed her arm around his shoulders and pushed him through the Capitol building exit. "Popé brought the pueblos together. Let us not you and I fight," she said.

"Our nation's government is not so stupid after all. The U.S. has redeemed itself, in my eyes, by putting up a statue to a man such as Popé," he said.

12

They camped at Cherry Hill Park, the closest campground to Washington D.C. Both seemed more relaxed since their journey began. She talked and laughed on her cell phone with Steve.

He smoked his ceremonial pipe, closing his eyes, obviously savoring the tobacco.

They had eaten well, thanks to their promised grant from NAG-PRA.

"Read me more tales of the man whose fascination with Pecos endangered his soul," he said.

He would never understand basic concepts of archaeology. She rolled her eyes and opened the diary, holding the pages up to the light.

"August 17, 1915.

Given the brutality of what happened here when the Indians finally rebelled against the Spanish after so many years of oppression, we believe the church wall is from the rebuilding after the Spanish returned in 1692. I'm not Catholic, yet I was moved by the jagged ruins of this ancient church, and fell to my knees, bowed my head, and said a prayer for the priests who were murdered here in 1680 when the Indians rose up against the Spanish."

"The priests who were murdered there," Grandfather said, mockingly.

"Sh. He goes on to talk about the Spanish Inquisition."

"My historian tells me the war between church and state escalated as the Inquisition tightened its grip, making lives miserable for both the Indians and Spanish settlers, but especially the Indians. The Puebloans often ran for their lives, leaving behind all their possessions, except for turkeys bundled beneath their arms and their precious sacred feathers. Often the friars chopped off their hair as punishment for idolatry. Fray Alonso de Posada, Head Agent of the Inquisition stationed at Pecos from 1662 to 1665, commanded all friars to burn the Puebloans' religious masks, prayer sticks and idols. He outlawed their Kachina dances. Fray Juan Bernal, Agent of the Inquisition, lived at Pecos from 1669 to 1671, as did Agent Fray Pedro de Ayala in 1673.

The Indians were not only victims of a religious war with the Inquisition but were caught in the middle of a battle between Governor and church. Governors often threatened Indians with death if they did not testify against their missionary when the governor went before the Inquisition and accused friars of fornication or some other blasphemy.

Among all this jealousy and hatred between church and state, the Indians questioned the Spaniards' god, who did not allow them to sing their songs and prohibited their sacred ceremonies so that their world turned upside down; the rains ceased and their crops failed. Their own gods no longer blessed them and punished them for turning to the Spanish god. Nor could the Spanish protect them any longer from the Apaches who ravaged their lands, murdered, kidnapped and pillaged both settlers and Puebloans.

Pecos was the best off of the pueblos, being friends with the Apaches and their joint trade fair. It seemed Pecos was the only pueblo spared from famine that swept across the land, during which even some of the Spanish had to roast cowhide to survive.

By 1680, the Indians blamed the Spanish for their troubles and the years-long drought. They were better off before they deserted their gods.

Small rebellions sprang up over the previous two decades and many Indians hung, but in lieu of the 1675 witchcraft trials, New Mexico was ripe for a major Revolt.

Oranges from Stanford arrived yesterday. "

Grandfather was asleep, with his chin on his chest, snoring lightly.

She nudged him gently and helped him to bed, tucking him in like a child.

"Did I miss the war?" he said.

"Just the seeds," she said.

"From one seed can grow a stalk of disenchantment. Two seeds planted in the same hole can branch out in a gnarly fashion that chokes the roots beneath. Granddaughter, I no longer wish to cross knives with you."

"Nor do I; your knife is more like a sword."

"As is yours, many times you have cut me to the quick," he said. "I have had a grand fencing master."

"Let us bury the tomahawk then. I am too old and weary, and you have a face as ugly as an ogre Kachina when you are mad."

"Fine, let's bury the hatchet," she said, yanking the covers up to his chin and slamming the camper doors.

She opened the driver's truck door and adjusted the overhead light so it would stay on when the door was closed, revealing her key in the ignition for anyone who was interested in stealing her truck and him.

She marched to the bathroom to shower, thinking the old buzzard would never change and examining her face in the mirror with flashing eyes. Ugh. He said she was ugly. Why did his opinion matter so much? He should talk. He looked like an ogre, even when not pissed off. Was he ever young and good looking? He must have sprouted as a troll. If she was hideous, it was his fault.

The cool water from the shower finally abated her anger.

She turned off the water, shoved her arms into her robe and sprinted, soaking wet, to the camper.

She sobbed with relief that her truck was still there with him sleeping in the back, and she wouldn't have to issue an Amber Alert—he could be so childish.

She removed her keys from the ignition and snapped off the overhead light.

She ran back to the bathroom, hoping no one had stolen her clothes.

He was right. She was pretty ugly when mad.

13

By the time she swung the bathroom door open at Cherry Hill Camp, her skin had air-dried. She wiggled into her pajamas and carried her damp robe over her arm, shivering and hurrying to the camper.

In the distance, a woman danced on the sidewalk, twirling a dream catcher around her wrist, sweeping the net across her head. Images twirled from the hole in the middle of the dream catcher and at first she thought someone had broken into her camper after all but the woman was Native American, clothed in a buckskin dress and moccasins.

Suddenly, the sidewalk buckled; the concrete faded in and out.

Magic created a dynamic dream catcher indeed, sending her day-dreams.

She spun around and vomited on a dirt road.

Ten men clothed in dark-blue hooded robes walked the dusty road with large wooden crucifixes bouncing against their knees. It seemed the earth parted as all jumped from the road to let them pass.

The Franciscan friars traveled so close to her, their robes brushed against her ankles. These men had the harshest faces. Lines of absolute power dug into their cheeks. Their eyes glowed with self-righteousness and their chins thrust out in defiance of all but their own cardinal law. Even their leather sandals pounded the road with the confidence of wild stallions. They behaved as men on a mission.

She kept her head down to avoid their piercing eyes and followed discreetly behind to San Miguel Chapel in old Santa Fe.

A tall, thin friar swaggered from the church, lifting his hand in blessing and greeting the other friars. This man wore a black hooded robe, his hands clasped in the wide arms. He appeared to float on the dusty road. The sun shone on his bald head that had a ring of blondish hair like a halo. There were deep marks on the sides of his pock-marked face, but the marks were fresh, like he indulged in self-flagellation as a religious fanatic and whipped his skin mercilessly with branches so sharp, the cuts looked like a razor blade sliced across his skin. Blood oozed from his face. Lavender-colored, spider-like veins protruded from his cheeks. A cross of ashes smudged his forehead. Specks of blood splattered across his chin and his robe, and dribbled down his neck. Teeth marks outlined his bottom lip which bled profusely. His chest rose up and down and something like a growl escaped his lips so that his spectacles vibrated on the bridge of his nose.

He jerked his hood up over his head so only a black hole was visible because he held his head back like a cobra about to strike.

With her head bowed she shuffled behind the friars to the back of the church where a group of Indians huddled, their wrists tied together. Armed soldiers guarded the prisoners.

A crowd of mainly Indians gathered at the fringes and looked down at the ground, avoiding the Franciscans' eyes.

The faceless friar in the blood-stained robe pointed to one of the Indians.

A soldier shoved him and he landed on his knees. The Indian bowed his head, his black hair sweeping the dirt.

"You are guilty of missing mass yesterday. Fifty lashings," the friar said, sounding like fingernails clawing a chalkboard.

The Indian didn't protest when a soldier ripped off his shirt, tied him to a tree and whipped him.

"You there," the friar said, pointing to another Indian.

The soldier pushed him forward to his knees and he cried out holding his leg in pain.

"I've done nothing wrong, Fray Bernal. I attended mass yesterday."

"You did not sing. Nor did you appear mournful during Communion. How can you save your soul if you do not fulfill your duty? Forty lashings," he said, holding up four fingers.

The sound of wheels on the nearby road diverted everyone's attention. Five wagons pulled up behind the church. Bars enclosed the wagon beds. Each cage held ten Indians, except the last cage which held only seven prisoners.

The wagons attracted a larger crowd who drifted into the arena behind San Miguel Church. Spanish soldiers, businessmen, ranchers, women and children all gawked at the caged Indians. A festive air crackled about the Spanish while groups of Puebloans huddled together at the fringes with wide eyes and hands grasped behind their backs, their faces flushed with fear. From their terrified faces it was apparent the friar with the freshly scarred face was head Agent of the Inquisition. His name Juan Bernal stationed at Pecos, rushed through the Indian crowd like the crack of a whip.

Fray Bernal smiled and held his hands up like everyone was a friend.

"These forty-seven prisoners are medicine men the Holy Office arrested for sorcery. Seven are to be hung each day," he said.

"What is their crime besides the fact that they are healers?" one Indian said.

The other Indians scurried away from him so that he stood alone.

"Where are you from?" Fray Bernal hissed.

"San Juan. I see among the healers my countryman El Popé. The healer saved my son's life by removing a stone from his throat."

Hollow-Woman jerked her head to a man who gripped the cage bars so tightly, his knuckles turned white. Like the other prisoners, he had been severely beaten yet there was such a supernatural glow about him, he seemed to tower above the others, though he was but medium height and wiry. Muscles bulged from his arms. Swelling on his face and bruises on his skin could not disguise his good looks, nor could cuts above his eyes hide intelligence that sparkled there. Like the other medicine men, the Inquisition chopped off his hair in punishment for idolatry. His reputation was legendary but he bled like any man. His knuckles were white since he clenched the bars; it seemed, to keep from falling. Or perhaps all the blood drained from his hands because he fought back. His hands were swollen, bruised, scraped, yet he did not cry out in pain. From the look on his dark face, he may have broken his hands on a few Spanish heads but they could not break his spirit. His hatred was so palpable; it was odd the friars did not sense his threat. The friars, in their arrogance, apparently believed God cheered for their side.

Fray Bernal slithered closer to the man from San Juan who dared defend Popé. Fray Bernal had no lips yet foam bubbled from the black hole of his hood.

"Your El Popé is no healer but a brujo. Your witch from San Juan seduced Fray Duran with the sole intention of recruiting the good friar as the devil's disciple. Fray Duran then butchered his entire family. You are Popé's disciple. You hide wooden Kachina images in your home and keep feathers for mischief of the foulest sort."

"No," the man said, taking a step back.

"Over here. Turpentine," Fray Bernal screeched.

He lit a torch, waving the flame around his hood encircling him like a fiery halo.

"Don't burn him," she yelled.

Fray Bernal's robe lashed against her bare calves though he stood some distance from her. His robe was made of material like a hairshirt, yet his robe felt slimy like snakeskin.

He seemed to glide as he moved towards her. His reddish eyes peered out of his hood from spectacles, proving he had his flaws even though he judged others like he was God.

He pointed at her and his fingernail advanced like a claw.

He splashed a bucket of turpentine on her bare feet and dangled his torch closer until flames licked her legs and the tips of her eyelashes glowed fiery-orange.

She screamed and a loud moan came from the closest cage. Popé's face filled with suffering, it seemed, for her. His hand reached through the cage bars. He was too far to reach her, yet his comforting touch stroked her cheek.

An Indian in the crowd grabbed a blanket and beat her feet until he extinguished the fire. He held her by her arm pits and supported her. She clenched her teeth to keep from screaming; afraid to draw attention else Fray Bernal might finish the job.

He seemed to grow two feet and cast an ominous shadow as he swirled around the square, his robe flowing behind him, his arms spread like a flying crow.

"Ten missionaries have died from mysterious causes and even more settlers have sickened. These so-called medicine men confessed to witchcraft. Throw the witches into their cells and let the trials begin," he said, lifting his neck and screaming like a mad man.

The Inquisition had severely beaten the medicine men, young and old, so most had to be helped to their jail cells.

Soldiers threw the men into seven adobe cells that encircled the church courtyard.

Heavy doors slammed shut behind them and iron locks snapped into place.

A soldier dragged a medicine man from the first cell.

Fray Bernal accused him of witchcraft.

A soldier twisted a rope around his neck and hung him from a tree.

The rope did not humanely break his neck and so he lingered, his moccasins kicking in the air, his face turning blue.

God, end his suffering. She stood there in the crowd, clasping her hands in prayer.

Finally, he expelled his body fluids, his body stilled and his choking sounds quieted to an eerie silence.

The other Indians moaned, and the Spanish clapped.

Fray Bernal repeated the atrocity until seven corpses swayed from branches, their moccasins pointed at the earth, their heads touching between their shoulder blades.

Oh God. She sickened and slapped her hand across her mouth.

A soldier led a naked Indian woman from San Miguel Chapel by a chain around her neck. She staggered about, yet managed to hide her breasts with her tangled hair but couldn't hide her shame. From her swollen, purple lips she muttered an oath in Towa and was apparently from Pecos or Jemez, perhaps an ancestor.

The woman's suffering exposed her soul. Oh, God, not just her soul; she hemorrhaged between her legs and bled from her bruised woman's spot which swelled and bore witness that her interrogators brutally raped her. These agents of the Inquisition, Franciscan friars who claimed to practice celibacy, perhaps saw her as a field animal instead of a woman, so in their eyes did not break their covenant with God by forcing her to have sex with them.

The woman swung her head to a noise coming from one of the cells.

Popé stared out from the window bars. His head seemed to shrink. He sounded like he strangled. Finally, the words he choked on erupted from his mouth and he screamed in Towa at the woman. "Angeni, stay strong my Love. I will come for you and save you. I will turn into a hawk and fly from this prison. My fingers may be broken but my wings are not."

Angeni did not acknowledge Popé. She lifted her heavy head to two Spanish officials who stood beside Fray Bernal. They all tapped their boots against the dirt like they were impatient for these festivities to end so they could get on with more important business.

"Francisco Xavier," Angeni said.

The dandy cocked his head.

"Diego López Sambrano," she said, wheezing and appearing faint.

Sambrano stroked his beard and smiled mockingly at her.

"I beseech you both as my husband's enemies and compassionate men, release Popé; he has done nothing wrong," she pleaded in Spanish

"Your husband will hang tomorrow," the men sang in unison.

Angeni turned her heavy head towards his jail cell, reaching out a hand to Popé. She stumbled and fell. Her buttocks hit the ground with such a loud thud, she split open and blood gushed from between her legs like the parted Red Sea.

Within moments…her head fell forward, her body lay limp and her eyes remained open, unblinking.

"Behold this lesson to any who harbor a witch," Xavier and Sambrano said, pointing at the dead Angeni.

Suddenly, a hawk swooped from the sky with talons drawn and dug out Sambrano's eyes.

Xavier dodged; swinging his head and protecting himself with his arms so the hawk merely scraped a claw across his wrist.

Chaos followed the blinding of Sambrano and attack on Xavier therefore, no Spaniard witnessed the hawk fly back to the second jail cell.

Hollow-Woman peeked though the bars of Popé's cell. He lay on the floor breathing heavily. His beak-like nose melted back into a human nose, and the feathers on his arms and legs dissolved back into his skin. A howl came from his throat and he rocked in a fetus position.

She had witnessed Grandfather shapeshift and knew Popé could have maintained his transformation for only a few minutes because of his weakened condition from the beatings. She wished with all her heart Grandfather had taught her the secret of shape-shifting; she would transform into a robin, fly through the cage bars and comfort him.

"Tomorrow the witches from the second cell will hang," Fray Bernal roared.

A thunder blast followed his words and grinning teeth appeared in his faceless hood.

A fellow prisoner whispered, "Do you hear that, El Popé? Tomorrow you will join Angeni and Masawkatsina will welcome you. This is why the sky darkened and she has not become one with the cloud people. Angeni waits for you, my friend."

Popé mewed, thrashing about the floor in agony.

"Perhaps we'll not hang tomorrow. I hear the pueblos are restless because of our arrest. The people will not forget their medicine men," another inmate whispered.

The crowd dispersed and she followed some Indians to the Governor's Palace, where a greater number had gathered, including a few hundred Tewa warriors from the north. Their numbers were so many that some defiantly stepped onto the long covered porch seeking dryness from the rain. A sign proclaimed Governor Juan Francisco de Treviño, appointed governor of New Mexico, 1675.

The Indians chanted, and yelled, and raised their fists.

"Our sorcerers and priests are in jail and will hang. Who then will stand between us and the dark spirits?" they said.

"Who will protect us from the power of the owl feather and black corn?"

The armed warriors threatened to kill Governor Treviño and every Hispaño if they did not release their sorcerers. Now!

The governor cowered in his palace while Capitán Sanchez swaggered on the flat rooftop, surrounded by a dozen armed soldiers.

Hollow-Woman leaned against a tree in the plaza yet the branches didn't cool her burnt feet.

A couple of soldiers with pale faces shivered beside her. One soldier held the butt of his rifle with a trembling hand. She cocked her ear to their conversation.

"In all of Nuevo México we are but two thousand, including women and children. How can we stop seventeen-thousand Indians if they all rebel? Treviño is insane, agreeing with the Inquisition to arrest all their medicine men."

"Let's just hope Treviño isn't as dumb as he looks. Most of the army is off chasing Apaches."

"Shush now. There's the Capítan. Let us hear what he has to say."

Sanchez spread his legs wide and waved his hands to shush the crowd.

"Our Royal Governor Juan Francisco Treviño, head of Nuevo México by order of His Majesty, is a just man who has only the good of the Puebloans in his heart. He has therefore decided to release your medicine men since you rely on these men as...uh...doctors... of sorts."

The captain spun on his heels and the soldiers marched from the roof in pompous fashion.

The medicine men were released and they drifted from their jail cells. Two Indians carried one man on a litter. His corpse joggled on the blanket. He must not have heard the rumors of impending rebellion and committed suicide rather than endure a hanging.

She returned to San Miguel Chapel and hid beside the wall.

Popé knelt beside Angeni's body. He wrapped his wife in a blanket and lifted her corpse in his arms. He hugged her to his chest and her head fell back. The Inquisition had severely beaten his back, but his wife's weight in his arms seemed to strengthen him and his muscles bulged as he rose to his feet.

She followed a distance behind him towards the Sangre de Cristo Mountains.

The sun shone its rays on their faces then began its slow descent to the west.

The Pecos Pueblo rose up from the earth to greet them just as the sun fell behind their backs.

Stars sparkled in the sky and a full moon shone down upon Popé and Angeni.

She quietly climbed a tree and sat hugging her knees to her chest.

He laid his wife's body down beside a mound of earth and dug with his fingers, unmindful of pain to his broken hand. He dug up a shallow grave and exposed a small skeleton with bony hands crossed below its neck.

"I bring you back, Angeni, like I promised to the land of your birth and bury you with our little Patomon," he said, cupping his wife's cheek with his hand.

Patomon means raging and the word spilled from his lips like a volcano. The flesh had fallen from his son's bones. A skeleton, the size of a three-year-old, lay in the shallow grave. His son may have died from Spanish diseases the Indians talked about at the Santa Fe plaza, probably mountain fever, measles, or smallpox, diseases which had killed so many other Indians. If true, then Popé had even more reason to hate the Spanish.

He cradled his wife and stepped into the grave. He gently laid her in the red earth.

"How can I live without my angel," he yelled, beating his heart with his fist.

He fell to his knees in the shallow grave and wrapped his arms around both his wife and son. Tears dampened his face and he rubbed his cheek against her hair.

He stayed in that hole until Hollow-Woman's knees stiffened, making it hazardous for her to climb down from the tree.

Rigor mortis set in so he had to break Angeni's hands from her wrists to break free.

He climbed from the grave and waved her hands in the air.

"Your gentle hands could once soothe my rage, but your hands are now brittle. There is no longer a reason for me to live."

His shoulders shook with sobs and he appeared a broken man.

Thunder boomed in the sky above his head and lightning illuminated Popé. He no longer appeared broken but whole. Even his hands were straight and no longer swollen. He clung to his wife's hands and lowered his brows.

"When a man no longer fears death, he is set free. Love breathes life into a man's heart, but then so does hatred and revenge, as a father, as a husband and as a man," he growled, showing his teeth like a wolf.

His snarl jolted Hollow-Woman back to Cherry Hill Park and she blew her nose on the arm of her robe, fully awake now and sitting on the sidewalk outside the bathroom.

She stumbled to the camper and lay there thinking about Popé, seeing his statue in her mind's eye; his apprehensive look and open nostrils as if he smelled an enemy. Her heart went out to this hero of the people because he was all too human. He was a man who suffered the pain of losing a beloved wife and child.

Her dream catcher spun from the ceiling and seduced her so her eyelids grew heavy. Her brain numbed. Nonsensical, disjointed thoughts drifted in and out of her consciousness.

And in the background…an image of a flattened corpse made her body jerk against the mattress.

She could tell by the air hitting her face that her dream catcher spun wildly above her. The smell of tree sap snaked through her nostrils. She stared cross-eyed with her nose pressed up against the bark of a tree and peeked around the trunk. The sun ricocheted off the adobe of a pueblo that appeared made of gold. Ah, one of the fabled golden cities of Cibola. The Taos Pueblo was the most rigid, strict, and conservative of all pueblos. In her previous nightmare, soldiers whispered that Taos had a history of bad relations with Spain.

Even in present day rumors circulated Taos Mountain had magical energy and watched over and protected the pueblo. Now, Taos Mountain rose from the back of the pueblo. In this dream world, Taos Mountain had lavender-colored eyes that drooped from the sun's warmth shining on the face of the mountain.

Taos Mountain opened its mouth and yawned.

From the sacred Blue Lake, a stream gurgled and divided the pueblo. Popé stood arrogantly by the stream with his chin thrust out and his fists clenched tight. His face was the color of roughened bronze, his profile strong and proud.

His black hair bounced on his head as he hurried along the bank of the stream and looked to the left and then to the right.

Another Indian she recognized from her last dream, climbed down from an apartment building and shook hands with him.

"Welcome back home, El Popé."

"Is there any word, Catiti?"

"The release of our medicine men from the Inquisition has revealed the Spanish weakness. Our enemy is vulnerable. Neighboring Apaches will join us."

"I prayed in the kiva and the god Pohéyemo appeared to me. 'You are my representative. Kill the Spaniards and destroy their symbols of Christianity,' Pohéyemo said. 'Return my people to the old ways.' No longer do I follow the Middle Path, Catiti. I will wait until the gods tell me the time is right. In the meantime, appoint a war captain from each pueblo and among the Apache tribes. Order all to take a vow of secrecy," Popé said with glowing eyes.

"I'll ask each pueblo to appoint their best war captain. We must hide you, El Popé. Francisco Xavier promises not to rest until you are dead. When you and our other medicine men were arrested, the Spanish attacked Taos. The kivas were raided and all the pueblos stripped of religious possessions. The people cry over the ashes and remains of destroyed Kachina masks."

"Ah, our sacred masks were passed down through generations and are irreplaceable."

She followed discreetly behind the two men.

Circles of rocks were piled at the openings where the kivas had existed. Now, burnt logs were stacked in the center of each circle. However, the Spanish failed to destroy one kiva.

Catiti led him to a hidden kiva where he climbed down a ladder and vanished below the earth.

Catiti then pulled the ladder from the kiva.

She left her hiding place behind a tree and peered into the hole. It must have rained earlier. Her feet slipped on the mud, and she tumbled into the kiva, landing in the soft, cool dirt but luck fell with her. Popé neither noticed her nor heard her scream; he appeared in a trance.

She curled up like a dead cockroach in a dark corner, and hugged her knees. Grandfather wouldn't even let her enter the dormant kivas at Pecos, much less a working kiva, her being a woman and all. She glared out at the darkness to a flame glowing in the fire pit. The ventilator shaft was only partially open to help conceal the kiva. Consequently, her eyes stung from the smoke.

Popé stared straight ahead with his eyes unblinking. He rubbed his hands over the small hole in the dirt that represents Shipapu where the gods live.

Suddenly, water bubbled from the hole and water spread out into the kiva.

She pushed herself against the dirt wall and breathed a sigh of relief when the water stopped spreading, leaving an eight-foot embankment around the kiva.

He held his hands above the pool of water and chanted.

The pool glowed golden in color then flashed to a blinding light.

The light dimmed and a man rose from the water. The man was made of mud.

How...? She rubbed her eyes but there he was still, Mudhead. Popé actually summoned the mud god.

Mudhead is a Katsina or Kachina as Katsinam are called by the modern Indian. Her Kachina collection included a miniature wooden image of Mudhead, but this Mudhead was not made of wood nor was he miniature; this being was made of damp, reddish-brown earth. He stood to his feet, the size of a full grown human man. Mudhead appeared like in her collection, to be constructed from clay by a child and had two mud circles for eyes and another small mud circle for his mouth so he seemed to be saying ooh.

Mudhead staggered on rubbery legs because the gods walked the earth many centuries ago so his legs were rusty.

During countless ceremonies costumed men, disguised as Kachinas, climbed the ladders and ran charging from the kivas. On these magical evenings, the people truly believed they witnessed the gods summoned from Shipapu.

Many times, Mudhead danced among those costumed men, at least a man pretending to be Mudhead climbed from the kiva to dance and mingle with the people during sacred ceremonies. As a child, she believed the masquerader was really Mudhead until Grandfather boarded her up at St. Mary's, and the older girls told her the Mudhead in the ceremonies was a fake. The masquerader's skin was plastered with dried mud, and he wore the same wooden mask over his head as the figurine in her living room. She had felt foolish, angry and letdown because the old man told lies.

The real Mudhead now shook his head and splattered her nightgown with mud. His shaking like a dog cleaned the mud from his purple skirt and matching socks that brushed his knees. In one hand, Mudhead held a feather that dried to fluff.

He walked with squishy movements on reddish-brown mud boots towards her.

She flattened against the wall, cringing.

I mustn't draw attention to myself. Mudhead is a warrior who speaks for the ancient ones and is extremely dangerous.

A bump of mud protruded from the top of his head and a decorative ring encircled the bump. The feet of Spanish soldiers were imprinted on his head, along with boots and spurs. Mudhead forged a connection over whoever stomped these footprints in the earth. With the footprints, Popé could track the Spanish so he could keep an eye on his enemy while he hid in the kiva and bided his time, making war plans.

Mudhead ignored her and sat on the ground, his muddy buttocks squishing and sounding like he shit.

Popé summoned another Kachina, and water gushed from the center of the pool and cascaded downward.

A dark head and muscular body glowing like copper formed in the waterfall and with one huge splash, Masawkatsina stood in the pool of water, ankle deep, in all his naked glory.

Popé probably summoned the Keeper of the Dead to raise a corpse army of invincible warriors.

Her throat itched from the smoke in the kiva. It took all her self-control not to cough.

Once more Popé held his hands over Shipapu and the pool of water glowed red.

A gurgling noise vibrated from beneath. Bubbles of life floated on top. A body swished in the water. An alligator-like head rose to the surface and snapped at the air.

The alligator-like man rose from the water and walked up the embankment.

Popé had summoned his third Kachina, the punisher Yowi, an ogre with a man's arms and legs, combined with the head and sharp teeth of an alligator.

She drew her knees up further to her chest and shuddered. Grandfather had promised Yowi would punish her.

Yowi stood to his feet, not wooden like her Kachina doll but flesh and blood. He opened his alligator mouth, exposing sharp teeth like rows of razor blades. He swung Fray Bernal's severed head from his hand. A monk's hood hung from the raggedy neck of the agent of the Inquisition. There were bloody marks on the cheeks, like the man had whipped himself.

Fray Bernal opened his eyes, and winked at her, and she almost lost it.

I should have kept my damned mouth shut. Ugh, I'm going to die.

Yowi cocked his alligator head in her direction.

She slammed her head against the kiva wall and clawed at the dirt, gasping.

Something sharp stroked her cheek.

Yowi's alligator-like face grinned at her, his teeth white and big.

Oh, God, I've got to get out of here. Where's the ladder? Dammit!

Yowi snuck up on her. He scraped her cheek with his knife. Each scrape moved closer to her neck. He growled low in his throat. Yowi planned to cut off her head.

Ah. Oh God. I'm not a priest. Please let me live.

Skeletons from the underworld must have followed Masawkatsina and stood behind him. Their skulls glowed in the dark and their red eye sockets glared at her.

"Kill the spy," a voice hissed.

"She is a woman!"

Popé moved quicker than lightning. He grabbed the knife from Yowi and sliced her throat.

Blood gurgled from her neck as her dream catcher hurtled her back to the present and the camper where she clung to the mattress with aching fingers.

Usually, her dream catcher spun around slower until it either changed directions or stopped spinning. But now...after spinning furiously the dream catcher hung perfectly still above her bed.

If one dies in a nightmare, then one dies in reality.

She grabbed at her jugular vein and sat up, staring at her dream catcher and waiting for Yowi to leap through the center.

Her eyelids slid like raw eggs down her cheekbones. She dropped to the mattress like a corpse and fell into a deep, deep sleep...which seemed to last only minutes because thick smoke awakened her. She grabbed for Grandfather, thinking the camper was on fire.

Suddenly, another nightmare sucked her in, thrusting her to the convento of the Pecos Mission, right at the front of the burning church. She screamed in an inferno and sweat poured down her face. Would her flesh cook until her meat was so tender, flesh melted from her bones?

Flames rushed up the adobe walls and shot from the roof. The west corner of the church crumbled from the fire.

There, at the door. Oh God. Someone burns.

A man dressed in sandals and the robe of a Franciscan stumbled from the church. His feet were aflame and the rosary around his neck burned. The metal cross melted on his stomach and he screamed as an Indian branded him. A cross made of flesh, outlined with cinders, steamed from his belly. Smoke waved about his fiery hood and flames shot out from his face.

All around the mission, Puebloans ran around with torches, whooping like wild Indians.

No. No! She tried to scream at them to stop. Savages! The friars are human beings. Don't cook them alive. They did horrible things to you to cause such anger but don't turn into them; be more humane.

A friar stumbled towards her with burning hands flung out. The smell of roasting flesh made her gag.

"Stay away. Leave me in peace," she said.

Coward, she berated herself. Why don't you help him? Think you're too good to get involved with the petty squabbles of the Pecos? Aren't you one of them?

Her eyes stung from smoke as the friar's robe burned to ashes. Flesh melted until a skeleton stood before her, its skeletal hands reaching out, its skeletal fingertips glowing red.

"Stay away. Leave me alone," she said.

Her feet sank into the blackened earth, imprisoning her legs.

The skeleton walked closer to her, so close, he placed his bony hands around her neck and choked her.

"Go with God, Child. You have my blessing in death. Your sins are forgiven. I have exorcised you," he hissed.

She woke up, gasping for air.

Her dream catcher no longer spun above the mattress but merely fluttered.

Within seconds her dream catcher spun clockwise.

She welcomed a happy dream as the wind whirled around the Pecos Pueblo and she felt herself sinking, until red dust covered her ankles. Tears on her cheeks plastered her face with mud. A biting wind dried the mud on her face to adobe and she stood once more in the ashes of a ghost pueblo.

She tried to pinch herself to awaken but her fingers were numb. She slept lightly, unaware of her heart pounding against her chest, as her dream catcher reversed directions to spin its darkness.

Ah, tricked her.

She opened her mouth to scream but no sound vibrated from her throat. She walked about the ghost pueblo, with her hands guiding her because of the blowing sand so she fell into the kiva hidden beneath the church ruins that Kidder discovered. Above her, priests screamed and heads chopped off, rolling around the floor like bowling balls. From the fiery smell it was apparent the church burned and the Pueblo Revolt still ravaged the earth.

She landed with a thud, the dirt cool on her butt cheeks.

She sat up, struggling to breathe in the deep kiva.

The sun began its ascent and cast the kiva in shadows…of ghosts.

She mewed.

Priests shuffled about on musty earth, clanking their rosary beads. Friars chanted and prayed and confessed.

The sun shined on the wall and ten robed, hooded shadows walked with their heads bowed.

The smell of burning flesh overwhelmed her and she cupped her hand to her mouth to keep from vomiting and fouling the sacred, religious kiva.

The chanting of the monk ghosts grew louder.

Something breathed down her nightgown and she flung out her hands and begged them to "please...please leave me alone."

Ugh! Cobwebs covered her hands and her fingers became entangled in a web.

Hot flesh reached out and touched her.

Fingers walked down her nightgown...up her nightgown.

Then suddenly it was just her and the bright sun now shining into the hole of the kiva.

Cowards! You leave at the light of day? Skulk about at night?

Drip, drip.

She spun around to a tomb in the corner.

The dripping sound echoed from blood creeping down the kiva walls.

The blood is Pecos blood, she realized.

The sun's rays shifted and shone brightly on the tomb, illuminating rust and cobwebs.

A big spider crawled along the lid of the tomb.

Creak.

The lid slowly lifted from the tomb.

She took a step back, another, and another until her fingers clawed at the earthen wall.

The lid of the tomb fell to the earth with a thud.

The kiva shook so hard, she landed on her back. A pain like someone took a knife and ripped open her spine caused her body to ripple. She broke her back and could not get up and run.

The words "Grand Inquisitor" wiggled across the tomb.

My God, it's Fray Bernal, the agent who ordered the hanging of the medicine men.

Fingers reached over the side and clenched the tomb, struggling to sit up.

The top of a head became visible.

An eye appeared, dead like an alligator's eye, his sharp nose and pointed teeth.

She screamed and woke up but her terror had been silent because Grandfather snored beside her.

The moon shone through the window, casting shadows in the camper.

She breathed a sigh of relief until her dream catcher began swinging.

She hugged the blanket and waited for Fray Bernal to climb from his tomb and leap from her nightmare, through the hole of the dream catcher, and onto the mattress.

She turned on her side and sobbed quietly, not wanting to wake the old man who at his age, needed his rest. Surely she would have died in her nightmare but her heart stopped and only kicked in again because of her body's natural instinct to live.

So Popé was a shapeshifter and transformed into a hawk to protect his wife.

There was once a witch by the name of Cienega, who possessed the body and soul of a beautiful woman from the Laguna Pueblo. During ninth grade Christmas break, Cienega swayed into their shack, like she didn't quite fit into her legs, giving the excuse that a peyote vision demanded she make love to Grandfather. Her voice slurred like she had difficulty making her lips work.

Hollow-Woman was so naïve at the age of fourteen that she believed Cienega about the peyote.

Grandfather growled and jumped on Cienega, knocking her down. By the time he locked his jaws around her throat, he transformed into a wolf and tore Cienega apart.

She jumped up and down, screaming, a young girl with spots of blood splattered on her white dress.

She became even more hysterical when the wolf turned to her, with sharp teeth bared and lips drenched in blood.

She jumped back, sure he meant to attack her next, but then the wolf transformed back into Grandfather.

He ordered her not to be afraid because he killed the shapeshifter who meant to harm her.

"Why would the shapeshifter wish to harm me?"

"Because she is jealous you may have inherited my gifts, but I never wished to burden you with the abilities of a sorceress and train you in the ways. My magic will be buried with me. Bah. You are nothing but a girl who will grow up to be a worthless woman."

She wished now he had trained her and honed her so-called powers. He seemed too old to protect her from Yowi or any other bogeymen her dream catcher conjured up. At his age, the exertion of shape shifting would probably kill him.

14

The next morning she stood over him with her hands clenched into fists. He sent her a dream during the day, never revealing his damned dream catcher might send her daydreams, which made her feel vulnerable in her waking hours. What a catastrophe if her dream catcher threw her back to the Seventeenth Century while she was driving.

"Don't you ever send me a daydream again," she said, her eyes narrowing.

"I did not send you a daydream," he said.

"But there was a woman holding a dream catcher and bringing me visions. I thought…"

"You say your dream catcher materialized when you were not sleeping?"

"Is that what she is, my dream catcher? I thought she was my… never mind what I thought. I only know what I saw."

"Ah, it is my fate for women to rain on my Kachina dance. While I was sleeping, this woman grabbed control of your dreams like the trickster Katsina Coyote. This dream catcher's magic is so strong, she searches you out. This is a very rare phenomenon for a dream catcher to masquerade as a human being and appear in a dream. If a dream catcher crosses over from the world of dreams to the world of reality, it does so for only one reason. Granddaughter," he said and took a troubling breath, "your dream catcher is not bringing you good dreams nor nightmares, but the endless dream of death."

The wind howled, sending shivers up her spine.

"Jesus! There you go again, scaring me," she said.

"I do not have Jesus Christ's fortune telling abilities but I tinker with the middle eye."

"Will you please shut up?"

"Maybe she's just trying to warn you of impending danger instead of kill you," he said, sounding conciliatory.

"Kill me?"

"Be careful on the roads today."

It was at that moment her truck wouldn't start.

She kicked the tires and cursed. She then lifted the hood and played around a bit, tightening nuts and bolts, adding water to the radiator. She got behind the wheel and carefully restarted, thinking the gas line was flooded.

She jumped down from the seat, slammed the truck door, lifted the hood and banged against the motor with a wrench.

He seemed amused by her battle. He held out his hands and hummed, casting off evil spirits.

"Hello, I could use some real magic here instead of your mumbo jumbo," she said.

"I can make a horse fly but this pile of metal has no soul," he said, shrugging his shoulders and walking away with a deep sigh. "I hope I do not live to see the day technology makes sorcery obsolete."

With a heavy heart, she called a tow truck to haul her pickup to the closest repair shop.

She punched in the numbers of NAGPRA and they told her to come in after lunch.

They decided to kill time by returning to the Capitol building.

They caught the number 83 city bus across from the office at Cherry Hill.

She blew her breath against the window and the glass fogged up. She wrote in the fog: Hollow-Woman was here!

She bounced on the springy seat and grabbed onto the bar in front of her.

They got off at the College Park Metro Station stop.

Neither of them had even traveled on a normal train, much less a subway train. She managed to buy fare tickets and maneuver their way around by badgering other passengers.

They caught the subway for the Federal Center SW Metro station, the closest stop to return to the Capitol building and Popé.

Once again they made their way to the National Statuary Hall and Grandfather excused himself and headed for the bathroom.

Remembering her dream, she walked behind the statue and counted the number of whip scars on Popé's back.

Her dream catcher must be working overtime and driving the mechanic who fixed her truck insane. A flash of the woman who masqueraded as her dream catcher turned the corner, her black hair flying behind her.

Hollow-Woman spun on her heel to follow, but Popé stepped from the podium and blocked her way. He still had a wide-eyed look, like he was astonished as she, that he was mobile but still made from pink Tennessee granite marble.

With his magic he showed her the war. One wave of his hand conjured upon the floor a vision of a skeleton army summoned by Masawkatsina. The skeletons rode skeletal horses to the rancheros and slaughtered Spanish men, women and children. They spared some of the women and took them captive, though most fainted at skeletons scooping them up into bony arms.

Yowi beheaded priests, while the Puebloans ran around with torches, setting the churches on fire, just like in her dream.

She smiled when Yowi beheaded the Agent of the Inquisition, Fray Bernal.

Yowi murdered Fray Velasco, Guardian of the convento at Pecos, along with young Fray Pedrosa.

With his sorcery, he showed one thousand Spanish survivors flee to the governor's palace in Santa Fe, their faces terrified in disbelief.

The Indians laid siege and cut off the water to Santa Fe.

Parts of the capital burned while the sun set and rose for seven days.

Atop Mudhead Katsina's head, footsteps appeared of sixteen hundred Spanish roaring out of Santa Fe, their horses' hooves squashing a few hundred Indians and capturing prisoners.

The remaining Puebloans scurried to kill the Spanish women they held captive in revenge for all the Indians who died in the rebellion.

Governor Otermín interrogated the captive Indians before ordering their slaughter.

On Mudhead, the indentation of wagon wheels, prints of horses' hooves, and petticoats swept across the mud. But nowhere was there an impression of a monk's robe across the Río Grande because the priests were all murdered by Yowi, whose alligator head rose from the river to cut them off.

Yowi snapped at other survivors escaping across the river.

He cut the bodies of some of the Spanish in half and the Río Grande ran red with blood.

While Franciscan friars writhed in agony, their faces scorched, their hair ablaze, a Spanish boy hugged the Lady, La Conquistadora, and burst through the church doors in Santa Fe. Her once magnificent dress blackened by fire, her golden-brown hair singed, her body swaying, her wooden eyes wide with fear, the Lady made it all the way to El Paso where the Spanish survivors cheered their Patrona.

The Lady's eyes drooped; her shoulders slumped with defeat, while the governor scratched his head, flabbergasted that the Puebloans would abandon God and their sovereign, King Charles II. The Spanish demanded vengeance and swore to wipe every trace of Indians off the face of New Mexico. The Lady's hands were held open to entreat them. Wasn't this what they were trying to do all along? Wipe out their culture, their language, their identity, all that made them Native American? Hadn't they learned anything at all, living among these people for more than a century? The expression in her painted eyes seemed to change to astonishment as she realized it was they who had wooden heads.

Then Popé switched focus to Santa Fe and Hollow-Woman watched the rebels raid the haciendas and the governor's palace.

The Spanish left behind a hoard of jewelry and Popé, dripping with Spanish jewels, resembled King Charles II as he rode triumphantly in Governor Otermin's carriage through the Santa Fe streets and the pueblos, waving at the people. His most royal Governor El Popé bounced in the carriage, his flesh melting from his bones until all that remained was a jeweled skeleton waving a skeletal hand at his subjects.

The booing of the crowd shocked her.

The images wilted until only Popé stood before her in the Statuary Hall, his shoulders slumped in defeat.

"No more Spanish lived in the lands of the people of the middle path because I led the warriors from the cornfields to rise up against the lions of Spain, who used us as work horses so we had little time to nourish our own crops. Our bellies were never full since the invaders came to our lands. Thousands died at their hands so, the death of some four hundred settlers was a small price to pay. I do not count the friars. The so-called holy men deserved to die. Yet, after the rebellion some of my people who before hailed me as the right hand of the god Po-héyemo, now labeled me a dictator and a tyrant, and compared me to the Spanish. Everything I did was for the pueblos. Tributes I demanded the people pay after the revolution were not paid with joy to honor me for freeing them from Spanish enslavement but instead, the people compared me to the invaders. The only model I had for governing was the Spanish, but I never captured Indian slaves nor shipped slaves on Spanish Galleons across the great waters. How could the people turn against me and call me the devil incarnate?" Popé said, sounding miles away from the confident leader in her dream the night before.

"No Puebloan could have made this work. Until you became governor of all, each pueblo had its own leader. It is not inherent in our people for one man to lead all the pueblos. This goes against all we believe in. Any man who does must wander far from the Middle Path to do so. Often great men aren't appreciated in their time. In your day, the people criticized you and were ungrateful, but your revolution was a great success."

"I had to rule with a firm hand to root out Catholicism and all things Spanish, to bring back the old ways so our gods would smile once more upon our people and lift the disease and famine ravaging our land. Their churches were destroyed. Ah, you should have seen the bonfire at the great cathedral at Pecos as flames danced upon the rooftop and vigas tumbled down like burning spears. When the flames were extinguished, all that stood were the walls, black as night, so we danced on the walls to loosen the adobe bricks and pushed and shoved, battering the walls with poles until the church tumbled into a mound of blocks."

"Yet, after freeing my people from the Spanish iron hand my jealous enemies blamed me when the rains did not come, instead of looking into their own black hearts. I told the people our gods would not bless the pueblos so long as there were those amongst us who still secretly worshipped the Spanish god," he said, sticking out his chin in a petulant manner, yet his eyes looked unsure and watery.

She insanely longed to pat him on his pink head.

"Your deeds were so great that even centuries after your death you are a hero to the Puebloans. Because of you, we are free to speak our languages. We still perform our ancient dances. We worship as we please. We have our Kachina priests and our sacred societies. Our kivas still exist and newborn souls can make their way from Shipapu into sunlight. Dead spirits are not trapped in the black lagoon beneath the earth and can exit the kivas to become cloud people and bring us rain," she said.

Peace settled across his face, and he climbed his podium, slowly turning back into cold marble.

It seemed he appeared not as wide-eyed as before, not so surprised that his spirit lived in the National Statuary Hall of Fame.

"Yipes! You scared the bejesus out of me," she said to Grandfather who patted her on the back.

"Who were you talking to?" he said, with twinkling eyes.

"No one," she mumbled.

"Ah, Popé's statue is so real it seems that at any moment he might come to life."

"What happened after the Spanish returned?" she said, dreading to hear of retaliation. If what happened at Acoma spilled Indian blood, she shuddered to think what the revolt spawned. Perhaps this was the real reason the earth glowed red at Pecos.

He looked down at the floor and sighed. "Let's leave this place; Popé stirs up painful memories. The scars on my soul dwarf the scars on his back."

They rode the bus to the offices of NAGPRA to pick up their paperwork.

"I shall wait here," he said and folded his arms across his chest, his cue for her not to argue. He leaned against the building, puffing on a cigarette, ignoring passersby who gawked at the Indian with wrinkled leather skin and high-top tennis shoes, and baggy jeans. On purpose, the old coot had put on a headdress of feathers. Give them what they want, he always told her. Don't argue with your betters.

Before she left him to confront NAGPRA, she whispered in his ear, "No one is better than you are, Governor."

He winked at her and laughed, like she finally discovered his contrary secret.

In very little time, she trotted out of the building waving the required paperwork to claim the bones.

"NAGPRA will pay all expenses to transport the bones back to Pecos," she said in a breathless voice. "We'll find a nice hotel. After all, NAGPRA is footing the bill. Had I known, we would not have camped, but they reimbursed us for our expenses so far. I understand the Marriott in Crystal City has a subway stop that goes right into a nearby shopping center so maybe we'll find a good steak house. Come on, Governor, let's go to lunch."

"I am in a mood for steak," he said, smacking his lips and rubbing his hands. He held out his fingers and happily took the papers which he hugged to his chest with a wondrous look upon his face. "This is more than a grant. This pile of tree shavings and ink means freedom for the missing ones to come home where they belong. Normally I hate the waste of trees, but in this instance the bark undertakes a great honor," he said.

They strolled down the street, arm-in-arm, like they were really somebody, her whistling a rowdy tune and him banging the ceremonial staff against the sidewalk.

15

The mechanic called with bad news about her truck, something about the timing chain and ruining the engine.

They rode the subway to Crystal City, as near to the National Mall as one could stay and rented a room at the Marriott.

Grandfather napped while she went to pick up their luggage and important stuff. She arranged for another repair shop to look at her truck for a second opinion.

When she returned, she rested for a short while then checked out the shops at Crystal City, without even having to go outside since an opening existed to the indoor mall from the Marriott.

She went back to the room and fetched Grandfather so they could walk to dinner at a nice seafood restaurant that had just opened up.

"All we catch is trout and catfish at home. I have never had pink fish such as this," he said, washing his meal down with white wine.

"It's salmon," she said.

"Ah, I must remember that name so I can ask Masawkatsina to serve it at dinner at my death celebration. The others will enjoy this fish."

"Actually," said the waiter as he poured another glass of wine. "Trout is part of the salmon family but salmon lives in the salty oceans rather than the fresh water of rivers." He bowed and left the bottle.

"To the bones," Grandfather said, toasting her. "They have lived near the salty ocean but will soon return to the valley of the Río Grande to join their brothers. They will have much to tell of their adventures. I can hardly wait to hear them speak of it."

"To the bones," she said, banging her glass against his.

He nudged her in the ribs, winked, wiggled his eyebrows and made her distract the waiter while he put the wine glass in his coat pocket.

He leaned on her as they walked back to the room.

"You should not have taken that glass," she said.

"As much as that wine cost it should include the glass. I could buy an entire bottle."

"Well it's not that cheap wine you drink; you could buy two bottles."

"And tell me of the wine of life; would you rather have just a sip or two bottles, though you pass out in your own vomit?"

She rolled her eyes at him.

"Here," he said when they entered their room. "I took this glass for you because you admired the craftsmanship."

"I never meant for you to steal it."

"How else can I give you a gift since you take all my money?"

He staggered across the carpet and passed out on his bed.

She removed his shoes and belt and covered him with a blanket.

All your money, she thought. All $65.00 a month doled out weekly to him else he would give it away the day after he got his check.

The time was going on six o'clock and she walked back to a gift shop and purchased a souvenir, stopping at a drug store to buy a magazine.

She sat at a café, sipping a cup of coffee and reading all the latest movie gossip.

Just before nine o'clock she returned to the room to find him sitting up in bed, his eyes bloodshot, a cigarette dangling from his mouth, and his hair sticking straight up from his head.

"Read me the diary of the man who shipped my bones across the country so they could see the great ocean," he said in a cloud of smoke and hiccupped.

"Drink," she said, twisting open a water bottle and handing it to him.

"I am parched because the wine grows grapes in my stomach, and I must water them," he said.

"You shouldn't smoke in the room," she said, pulling the diary from the leather case.

He grunted, blowing smoke in her face.

She glowered at him while he puffed away.

"August 27, 1915

My historian tells me that after Popé's death, twelve years after the revolt, the invaders returned in 1692 with a wise governor, Don Diego de Vargas, who began his reconquering with the mighty Pecos. He pardoned the pueblo in the name of King Charles II and promised no retaliation. The missionaries then forgave the Pecos Indians their sins and baptized all children born during church absence, with de Vargas acting as godfather.

Most of Pecos Pueblo wanted no more bloodshed and refused to join in a new plot to kill the colonists because de Vargas proved an honorable man and true Christian who promised to be a friend. In fact, he so impressed most of the warriors, they offered to fight at his side, if need be. The Pecos governor even sent him food while de Vargas bided his time outside Santa Fe, waiting for the right moment to recapture his Spanish capital. When he finally attacked, Pecos warriors joined him in his fight and helped him win back Santa Fe. In gratitude, de Vargas offered to defend the Pecos Pueblo when needed. Both sides often helped each other in skirmishes.

Pecos also hoped that once the rebellions died down, trade would prosper, which is why Juan de Ye took Apaches with him to welcome de Vargas. Both the Pecos and the Apaches invited the Spaniards to the Pecos Trade Fair held every October.

De Vargas hired Pecos carpenters to rebuild the governor's palace, other government buildings, and churches in Santa Fe. Two years after the Spanish returned they constructed the Pecos cathedral which ruins stand there today.

The Puebloans taught the Spanish a hard lesson with their revolt so the king abolished the encomíendas. The friars waited for the people to come to their God voluntarily."

"As the Mexicans say, you can lead a burro to water but you can't force it to drink," Grandfather said, slapping his knee and laughing heartily.

"It states in the diary that most of the Puebloans welcomed back the Spanish with open arms," she said.

"I imagine they missed Spanish food and conveniences of Spanish tools and way of life, more advanced than the times of the ancients. We all like our comforts, do we not? As I recall, when you came back from school as a child, you demanded a television and a radio and all the other things you missed when you lived with the nuns," he said.

"I don't remember ever asking for anything from you after you abandoned me to the nuns."

"It was for your own good."

"That's open to interpretation," she said, shrugging her shoulders.

"Read. Read, and do not interpret," he said.

"A second, smaller revolt erupted in 1696 and divided Pecos on the issue of helping Governor de Vargas. A vigilante group of Pecos Indians took by surprise five leaders who opposed de Vargas and executed them in a kiva. The pueblos of Picurís, Tanos and Taos wanted the rebellion and attacked Pecos, but de Vargas rallied to their aid. This bad business of Pecos killing Pecos ripped the pueblo in two. Things changed after that. A people who are torn apart from within cannot stand strong. Look at what happened between the Catholic Church and the Spanish government who nicked at each other's throats in the old days. Bad blood lingered after the inner fighting and some of the Pecos Indians moved out of the pueblo."

"Then we're not the last of the Pecos?" she said, dropping her jaw so her chin almost touched her chest.

"After more than three hundred years, the deserters' blood is so diluted they are no longer Pecos, even if any know of their ancestry. You and I, alone, are direct descendants of the people who toughed it out and stayed at Pecos until the end," he said.

"So with all this friendship with the Spanish government, what happened that Pecos failed so badly in the ensuing years?"

He pointed to the dream catcher.

Surprisingly, he had been sober enough to attach the dream catcher to the light fixture. He must have done it while she completed her business in the bathroom. Ugh! She felt like screaming.

"Why did you hang that thing above my bed?" she said.

"The story is not finished. That salmon does not stick to the ribs any better than trout sticks to its own skeletal frame. I am hungry," he said.

He played around with the phone, called room service and ordered him some dessert. He sat back, well satisfied like the deer that escaped the hunter's sights. "I could get used to living like the whites," he said.

He shoveled cake and ice cream in his mouth, grunting and chugging a glass of water.

He monopolized the bathroom for half an hour before coming to bed smiling and smelling of baby powder.

For the rest of the evening she lay against the pillows, playing with the remote.

He fell asleep holding a lit cigarette and she put it out in an ash tray, then soaked it with water, then shoved it down the disposal in the half-kitchen.

She gently closed the bathroom door and shimmied into her nightgown.

She tiptoed to her bed and dived beneath the covers. Ah, to sleep in a real bed all to herself.

"You will ship my mattress to Boston. You will not throw it away with the cooking stove and other junk," he said in a commanding voice.

"What?" she said, banging her head against the wall.

"I cannot rest where others' nightmares have haunted. I cannot take my repose where dreams have shattered. I cannot rest in the dark void of other heads. I make an exception tonight because you have had a disturbing day."

"How do you know the truck...?"

He flung his arms wide and caught some Z's while sleep eluded her. Just in case he was right and fixing her truck proved too expensive, the logistics of transporting his flea-bitten mattress was nightmarish.

She let out a heartfelt sigh and tried to get some rest with one eye open to the dream catcher, appearing exotic at the Marriott.

She turned on her back and slammed her arm across her eyes, blocking out the street light that shone through the curtains. Darkening the room with the zero-light curtains was not an option or else he might fall when he got up at night to pee.

Crap! From the other side of the room something glowed in the dark. The light grew brighter to reveal a skeleton, stark white, sitting in the corner on her suitcase. Her dream catcher whirled with a buzz, sending her one of those dreams where it feels like you're frigging half awake.

She removed her bed covers, and tiptoed over to her suitcase.

She dropped to her knees and stroked its skull.

The skeleton turned to her, like a cat might, purring.

She touched a hole in its ribcage and a jolt like electricity seeped through her body, followed by a cracking noise as an arrow entered the side of a warrior, about twenty years old.

A flash of lightning illuminated the room. A sharp pain jabbed her at the back of her neck and a whirlwind hurled her to Pecos, where she landed on a rooftop of the pueblo, holding in her arms a warrior with flesh on his bones. An arrow stuck out of his ribcage and he struggled to speak.

Tears flowed down her face as she brushed his hair back from his head and wiped the blood from his mouth.

"Who wounded you?" she said in a hoarse voice.

He pulled at her sleeve and lowered her ear to his lips. He spoke in Towa.

"In 1700, the Comanches muscled into New Mexico, attacking the Puebloans, the Apaches, and the Spanish. We are so isolated here at Pecos. At first, Spanish soldiers helped protect us but after fifty years, the Comanche butchers still attack; they are such fierce fighters. No one knows why they hate us and wish to crush us."

"Perhaps they aim to prove their superiority by vanquishing the mightiest pueblo," she said.

"We were the richest when we traded with the plains Indians our blankets, jewelry and pottery for their buffalo hides, shells and flints. Comanches warred with Apaches, our major supplier, for control of the trade. Comanches are the fiercest fighters and won. Comanches shun us and take their business to the Taos Trade Fair, making us poor and Taos rich. There is no longer a trade fair at Pecos."

"Shall I call for a priest?" she said, noting the cross dangling from his neck.

"Holy men come no more to Pecos. God sent the Comanches to steal our cattle and horses. They hide in the woods to ambush our hunters, gatherers and workers who are so scared they no longer work the farther fields or fish for trout. We keep close to the pueblo and go hungry. There are only 150 of us now. Their pursuit of our destruction is brutal," he said, closing his eyes.

She screamed as the warrior vanished from her arms, turning to a pile of dust.

She peeked over the side of the roof to where hundreds of Comanches walloped outside the perimeter, attempting to scale the pueblo walls.

She jerked her head back to her room at the Marriott. She still held the skeleton but he soon vanished from her arms, yet her dream catcher still hissed at her.

A chill crawled up her spine because someone moved about her room. She could see the bump on Grandfather's bed so knew he slept and took no part in her half-awake nightmare, only his magic participated. Besides, the noise came from the opposite end of the room.

She crossed her fingers and hoped she was really dreaming. Please, don't let it be a burglar, someone who overheard us at the restaurant discussing our grant.

A glowing light blocked her way to the bed.

As the light dimmed she could make out a woman's shape in the form of a transparent hologram so she could see right through her like a ghost.

Oh God, this is even worse than a break-in.

This woman spun her daydream; the masquerader who Grandfather claimed like the grim reaper, brought her death.

The woman dressed like the ancients and wore knee-length moccasins. A tanned leather skirt brushed her slender ankles encased by moccasins. Black braids bounced against her chest as she moved towards her. She appeared a frail wisp of a woman. As she got closer, this apparition seemed more heart-breaking than threatening. Her face looked vaguely familiar. She held a dream catcher in her hand that looked exactly like hers.

Oh, God, her dream catcher had not only personified but was going to speak to her.

"Smallpox and measles killed even more than the Comanches. The Pecos population declined as if the entire pueblo represented Job in the Bible," the woman said in a sing-song voice.

Light ricocheted against a jewel hanging from the woman's neck and stung her eyes, blinding her. The woman's face became fuzzy but she could still make out two gigantic tears that rolled down her cheeks. Somehow the woman hooked her own heart with hers along with her emotions. It felt as if the unhappiness of the world rested upon the woman's thin shoulders. Such grief overwhelmed Hollow-Woman; she floated in a void, her forehead flat against the woman's forehead, her eyes locked with her muddy brown eyes, their minds melding.

The woman's doe-like eyes swirled with liquid until one enormous tear dripped out the corner of each eye, slid down her cheeks and splashed against her necklace.

Hollow-Woman screamed as the woman unhooked her heart. The energy she took with her seemed to suck out her own energy to the point of exhaustion.

Hollow-Woman screeched, pointing at the woman's necklace and the five tips swirling around a heart-shaped stone. She searched for this necklace nearly all her life. This woman, this dream catcher, whose thin shoulders shuddered with tears, was her mother.

Hollow-Woman reached out a hand to her but the wind picked up her mother like a whirling tornado and tore at her flesh until a skeleton floated above. Her eye sockets sunk into her skull, her shoulder bones slumped, her mouth opened in a silent scream and her bony hand stretched out.

Before they could touch, the wind took her mother away with a bone crunching twist and she vanished through the hotel window.

Her mother's necklace and dream catcher swirled in the air and followed.

She felt such an overwhelming loss; she dropped to her knees and pushed her face to her thighs. Ah, she landed back in the present; her dream catcher stopped spinning above her bed. The hotel window was not broken and no glass on the carpet. Feeling disoriented, her pulse raced and her body was bathed in sweat. Did her mother's ghost really visit her?

Someone was crying out loud.

Her own tears were silent so she wouldn't wake the old man.

Moonlight streamed in through the window and two giant tears wobbled on the floor, sounding like a washing machine jiggling. These tears were not the ordinary tears of a woman but of a mystical being. The tears resembled a gelatin-like substance so she scooped up the tears with a spoon; the tears wiggled on the spoon, like clear Jell-O. She never touched another woman's tears before so, she reached out a fingertip...carefully...delicately...she stroked, marveling at their ten-. derness. The tears were not smooth like expected, but a rough grainy texture with flecks of red like they were nicked by shards of a broken heart. The feel of these tears was unlike anything she ever touched before, like a precious stone not of this earth. These were her mother's tears, no mere drops of fluid but pieces of her mother's ghost, straight from her transparent heart. The pieces were sturdy, pliable and bubbly, yet fragile. She could see right through to her mother's heartbreak.

She felt such overwhelming sadness for her mother, not just missing her, but thinking about her dying so young and her time on this earth cut so short. Her mother must have been awful young when she died, early twenties or perhaps a teenager.

She dropped the tears into a baggie and zipped the bag sealed, marking the baggie, with the hotel pen: Tears of a Dream Catcher.

Her mother masqueraded as her dream catcher and acted as her guide to the spirit world of Pecos, but Grandfather was wrong. Her mother did not send her the endless dream of death. Her mother would never hurt her.

The room spun dizzily and Hollow-Woman fell sideways and slumped to the carpet.

When she awoke some minutes later, or perhaps hours, she had one hell of a headache.

She couldn't remember walking back to her bed, but then she never left the bed since it was all a dream.

Her head felt a bit fuzzy.

There was something slick in her hand.

She held a baggie up to the sunlight and gasped at her half-asleep scribbling, which marked the bag, Tears of a Dream Catcher.

Tears are usually clear. This liquid was cloudy.

16

To kill time while waiting to hear about her truck, she hopped on the subway, leaving Grandfather to rest at the hotel.

After a short ride, the train doors opened for the Smithsonian Station stop.

The Natural History Museum should have a microscope.

The literature bragged the museum was the size of eighteen football fields, big enough to get lost in. She ended up in the basement and maneuvered through a haze of hallways, reserved for employees. That wide door appeared a way out; instead she stumbled upon thousands of skeletons, apparently human.

"May I help you?" a voice said in a New Orleans drawl. The young man peered at her from light grey eyes below a cocked eyebrow and more than a passing interest.

"What is all this?" she said, waving her arm around the room of skeletons and bones.

"Native American remains waiting for repatriation, only for tribes hoping to claim their ancestors; it's like looking for needles in a haystack. There are about 15,000 skeletons scattered about in these storerooms, all victims of science. The Indians want their relatives back, but finding out which ones are theirs...well look around and you can see the problem. I come in here on my breaks to escape the tourists and visit the poor souls."

"Who gathered these bones?"

"Private collectors who wanted to show off to their guests."

She made a face.

"And mostly in the 1800's, scientists wanted to prove that whites are superior. Ishi, the last surviving Yahi, was considered the last wild American Indian. Most of his relatives were massacred at Three Knolls and the remaining few hid for forty years until only he was left. Starvation caused him to wander, nearly naked, from the woods in northern California and hide in a slaughterhouse. He lived at the anthropology museum at Berkeley. Anthropologists studied him and gave him a home until he passed away in 1916."

"Yeah, Berkley gave him a home so they could dissect him after he died," she said.

"Yeah, it sucks. His brain was sent to the Smithsonian against Ishi's wish not to be autopsied."

"Did the Smithsonian want his brain because he was the last of his kind?" she said, opening her eyes wider.

"Nah, scientists were doing a comparison study of the size of brains of various races. The Smithsonian collected 300 brains in all and Ishi's was important since he was a representative of the Native American race."

"Kind of like the Nazis," she said.

"I hear Ishi's brain is in a Smithsonian warehouse in Maryland preserved in a sealed tank. Some tribe in California is trying to get his brain back to rebury his brain with his remains but they're not Yahi so it's tricky."

"I can imagine," she said, telling him a bit of her own story.

"Oh, wow, you can relate then. During the Indian Wars the Surgeon Generals ordered the army to send back skulls for scientific study; so soldiers beheaded bookoos of Native Americans and shipped their heads to D.C. Our government, also, paid good money to civilians who would bring in their bones," he said.

"My god, our government encouraged this?"

"If scientists didn't have to rob graves for specimens, they could spend more time studying disease from the samples and improving our health."

"Right, doing racial profiling of specimens' brains sure improves our health," she said with a wry smile.

"It wasn't just Berkeley who befriended natives to study them. The explorer Robert Peary met six Eskimos in Greenland. In 1897, they traveled to New York at his invitation. He turned them over to the anthropologist Franz Boas who moved them into the American Museum of Natural History in Manhattan. Four sickened and died. Unlike Ishi, these guys had family but Boas did not ship their remains back to their loved ones. Instead, he boiled the flesh off their bones so he and his colleagues could study their skeletons," he said.

"Oh, wow, you look pale, please don't throw up," he said, kindly offering her a chair. "I didn't mean to gross you out with Frankenstein stories." He sat across from her leaning forward and lowering his voice like he was about to reveal more horrors.

"One of the surviving Eskimos traveled back to Greenland and the other stayed in New York—a little fella named Minik, six or seven years old, whose father was one of the dead Eskimos. They even gave a pretend funeral and substituted a fur-wrapped log for his father's corpse, which the child walked behind, crying. Later, an older and wiser Minik discovered the hoax. It crushed him to visit the museum and see his father's bones displayed in a glass case. His story reminds me of yours except Minik spent his life trying to get his father's bones back from the museum that lied to him."

"Did Minik ever get back his father's bones?" she said, rubbing goose bumps on her arms.

"Nope. After Minik grew up, he moved back to Greenland for a bit and struggled with a language and culture he forgot. He returned to New York. The Spanish flu killed him in 1918. Minik was buried in New York City at his request, a place he came to love, even given the treachery of New Yorkers claiming to be his friend."

"What about his father's bones?"

"New York finally returned them to Greenland six years ago," he said, slapping his knees. "Well, I've got to get back to work."

"Do you mind if I stay here for a little while?" she said, eying a microscope on a table to her left.

"Hell, if I care; isn't my museum but don't stay long because my bosses try to categorize the bones when there's time, even though lack of documentation is a pain, I hear. There used to be more skeletons but some tribes have claimed about three thousand of them," he said.

"You'd think with all the DNA tests nowadays, they could find out who their descendants are and repatriate the bones that way," she said.

"That would be a frickin' nightmare. I hear that around the nation in museums, national parks services, universities, and other government agencies there's around two million Native American bones."

The blood rushed from her face, just as she began to feel more like herself.

"The only ones I've befriended are them four hundred skulls over there," he said, laughing. "They're from the Sand Creek Massacre that happened November 29, 1864."

He talked fast, reciting the facts of the massacre.

"If anyone comes in, just pretend you're lost. The way out is to the left, then two rights, then another left, then a right, then two lefts. Don't mention me, please," he said.

"I won't. Thank you for everything."

"I don't see many living Indians. Guess you all don't leave your lands much in case of grave robbers," he said, laughing.

He walked to the door, swinging a tool box, his sandy hair flopping.

She placed the cloudy Jell-O-like tears under the microscope and placed her eye to the lens.

Like bacteria, thousands of white...zeroing in on one speck...zooming out...what she thought of as bacteria was really...

"Well, I'll be damned," she said, her breath rushing out.

In each tear drop were piles of tiny skeletons.

Her head trembled when she placed her eye back on the microscope lens.

Slowly, from the lamp heat, her mother's tears melted.

No. No.

She clawed at the microscope light switch to cut off the heat source, but the tears dissolved. The tiny skeletons dissipated to calcium specks floating in the liquid.

She zipped the baggie shut and dropped it in her purse.

Now, the only skeletons were the human-size ones in this room.

She sighed and walked around the floor, sweeping up bones that must have belonged to a hand, dropping the bones in a box, collecting more unhinged skeletons, thighs, feet, and an arm. There was a chest, hip bones, and ass bones. Another set of bones, nearly a whole skeleton, languished in a corner, along with a breast bone, and an entire rib cage.

Butterflies fluttered in her stomach at shelf after shelf lined with coffin-shaped boxes stacked haphazardly to the ceiling. The words were barely readable on a seal glued to the side of a box because several boxes on the lower shelves twisted sideways. The faded print read: This side up. Store in a dark place. Caution. Fragile. Human Waste.

On the furthest shelf were coffin-shaped boxes, child-size, stacked to the ceiling.

She jerked open one of the file cabinets and cringed at piles of bones.

A child's skull stared at her from the table that held the Sand Creek Massacre collection. A lot of these skulls were child-sized but this one attracted her with its droopy eye sockets. The skull fit in the palm of her hand, and the wide-eye sockets seemed to sag even more. Who was this Cheyenne child; boy or girl? From the size of the skull, maybe six years old.

This child should have been buried in Colorado or Kansas so grass and flowers could grow over her and a tree could shade her in summer, a place where her parents could have visited from time to time; except, soldiers probably murdered her mother and father, right before her very eyes.

Grandfather said one should listen with one's heart, that the dead person's spirit lives in his bones. She hugged the skull to her chest, released her breath slowly and concentrated while rubbing a scar on the bony forehead. A feeling like a jolt of electricity streaked through her body and her hair stood on end like someone lifted a fork to her scalp. A vision appeared of a little girl, running in a circle with a group of children, laughing and screaming as they chased each other.

Hollow-Woman pressed her cheek against the child's skull and closed her eyes. Their encampment at Sand Creek blossomed before her. She was not transported to the scene like with her dream catcher, but could see through the child's eyes, as if inhabiting the little girl. The name Shy-Dove fluttered from the skull like a bone splinter.

Shy-Dove hid behind her mother's skirts and peeked out at the Chiefs Black Kettle, Niwot, and White Antelope who rode into camp and dismounted from their horses.

"All these battles because of the white man's gold, a curse upon our lands, have ended. The white man will have his gold and no longer disturb us. Let us feast tonight and celebrate the peace treaty we have made this morning at Camp Weld," Chief Black Kettle said.

She licked her chops.

The chiefs sent off the warriors to hunt, patting their backs and wishing them a bountiful return.

She and the other children—who stayed behind, besides the men too old to hunt and the women—ran behind the horses, waving at their backs. Her stomach grumbled as visions of elk meat danced in her head. She fell to the ground in mock ecstasy, rubbing her stomach and laughing with her friends.

Mama nursed baby brother, while grandparents gathered wood for the fires.

The adults sang while they worked no longer acting worried.

With her arm circled around her best friend, the two girls watched Chief Black Kettle put up the white man's flag.

He patted her head and Shy-Dove smiled back at him.

"The war is over, children. Colonel Chivington promised these stars and stripes will keep soldiers from attacking us. Now run along and play."

The wind flapped the flag about, sounding a bit like a drum.

Thunder pounded in the distance announcing the coming of a mighty storm.

Her heart pounded. Hundreds of men in blue uniforms charged towards the camp, some with rifles aimed and others with swords above their heads.

"The army tricked us. Quick! Gather the children together," Chief White Antelope yelled.

Black Kettle raised a white flag but still, the soldiers fired at their camp, splattering blood on the American flag.

She ran towards her family.

Bam!

A club bashed against Mama's skull.

"Mama," she screamed as blood spotted her dress.

Baby brother lay like a doll with a knife in his heart, his little legs fluttering, and blood oozing from his chest. He didn't even know how to walk yet, much less run from the soldiers.

Chief Black Kettle grabbed her around her waist and ran with her.

A soldier plunged a knife into his stomach and they both tumbled to the ground.

Her head banged on a rock and the camp spun around her. Blood gushed from her nose and she clamped a hand over her mouth and smothered her sobs like Mama taught her.

The chief of the soldiers had a beard, a moustache and a forehead like an egg because his hair grew so far from his eyebrows. His eyes burned like coals.

"Colonel Chivington? You," Chief Black Kettle said, holding his wounded stomach. In answer, Colonel Chivington twisted the blade of his knife and blood gurgled from his mouth. Chief Black Kettle lay there gasping, "When we signed the peace treaty you bragged what a Christian you are and a Methodist preacher who opposes the slavery of black men."

"Damn any man who sympathizes with Indians! I have come to kill Indians, and believe it is right and honorable to use any means under God's heaven to kill Indians," Chivington screamed.

The girl watched with dazed eyes the soldiers slice ears to be worn as earrings and chop off fingers to steal the rings.

A couple of soldiers kneeled at White Antelope's corpse and cut off his ears and his nose. One soldier chopped off his testicles and held them up, laughing. "I can make a tobacco pouch with these," he bragged.

The soldiers took their knives to foreheads. Father always said the Indian never knew about scalping a human being until the white man taught them.

They cut off noses, for souvenirs, a soldier said but the shouting and screams faded as her blood flowed. She felt only numbness, even as she watched soldiers scalp baby brother.

The soldiers lifted the women's skirts, even the old, and sliced off their private parts. Some of the women screamed so loudly, it unstopped her ears so she could hear.

"Remember, we need to send the skulls to Washington," Chivington said. He then pointed at some soldiers who took their knives to necks and sawed off the heads.

"Empty the tipis of everything you can sell," he ordered others.

Some soldiers loaded up the Cheyenne horses and rode off, while others burned the tipis.

Shy-Dove floated above her body, between smoke and the sun and a soldier kneeled by her side. He wiped a bloody knife on her skirt then the blade felt cold against her neck. She silently screamed in agony as the rough blade sawed against her skin in jagged lines.

Now the soldier waved her head from his hand, grinning. Jagged pieces of her neck appeared like someone ripped it from her shoulders.

She wanted to run from him but couldn't move her legs. Where are my legs? My pretty moccasins Mama made?

He set her head on his lap and took a knife to where her forehead met her scalp...

Hollow-Woman touched the scar on the small skull. Right there is where the child had hit her head. She kissed the damaged spot, then set the skull down and swallowed bile. Oh my god, Grandfather was right about the bones being alive so that would mean their spirits were aware when all the horror took place.

Which skull belonged to Chief Black Kettle and which skull was Chief White Antelope's?

She touched the dent of one skull and shuddered, feeling the blow of a club.

She rubbed the scar on the forehead of another and cringed at the jab of a knife.

Skulls stared expectantly at her with wide open sockets and teeth clenched in their skulls.

What do you want from me? What? What? Tell me! It was foolish talking to a bunch of skulls, even if it was only in her head. By the expressions on their face bones and sunken eye sockets, it seemed they begged a favor, but her plate already overflowed with the repatriation of her own people, some two thousand or so lost souls.

Their empty eye sockets disturbed her so she swung to the opposite corner where a skeletal hand reached out. She bowed and shook the bony hand. How do you do, sir or lady?

She lifted the hand and walked it over to a box.

She dropped the hand and screamed. The bones moved. God almighty and Jesus, the bones squeezed her hand...but now...now the bones just lay there in the box with bony fingers reaching out like the hand tried to touch the other bones.

Okay. Calm down. Don't panic. A hand so brittle cannot squeeze back else the bones would have shattered. The handshake is simply a figment of your imagination.

This room smelled like a freshly dug grave. It reminded her of a graveyard except the dead weren't buried beneath the ground. This was as creepy as pictures of the Holocaust and graves unburied revealing piles of skeletons thrown, like garbage, into one big hole.

She stifled her screams. She must leave. Now! These poor souls were so unhappy and restless they haunted her, whispering to her, pleading with her.

First left, then two rights. Next left. Right, then two lefts.

Breathless, she ran up the stairs, made her way to the exit and practically flew out the entrance to the subway stop.

When she got to the Marriott and her room, she glanced at the dresser mirror and shrieked because she looked like a scarecrow with grave dust in her hair and on her nose.

Grandfather sat alone on the edge of the bed, staring into space, his eyes rimmed red.

The feeling that she abandoned him crushed her, as she tore off her clothes and plunged into the shower. Water splashed across her face, mingling her tears with soap.

She slid down the shower wall, hugged her knees and cuffed her ears. The bones from the museum still cried out to her, pleading with her to take them home, screaming at her in pain.

She scrubbed her arms and her legs raw at the spots of Cherokee and Arapaho blood.

She jerked a comb threw her wet hair, vowing to never tell him about her tour of the Museum of Natural History or what she saw. Instead, she would tell him she visited the National Museum of the American Indian.

Oh, Jesus, why won't their blood come off?

She climbed back in the shower and lifted her face to the shower head. Water streamed down her face but did not wash the blood from the Sand Creek Massacre that splattered her soul.

She turned off the water, rested her head against the shower wall and breathed deeply.

From the look on his face when she first walked into the room, he must have seen the atrocities at Sand Creek and all those bones at the museum. From the beginning of their trip, he gazed through her eyes just like she peeked through Shy-Dove's eyes. His magic connected her to him; like that time he appeared at the Pecos Pueblo when she ran away from the nuns.

I am always watching you. Do not think that because you are away from me that I cannot see what you are up to, he had said.

She jerked her arms into her robe, sprinted to the bed, and hugged him.

They rocked, crying, but they never spoke a word.

17

She ordered room service for their lunch then picked at her food. He stood with his fists on his hips, glaring down at her plate.

Blah-blah-blah. His umpteenth lecture frazzled her nerves.

"Are you rested now?" she said, chomping one more bite to satisfy him.

"Never felt better." He stood with bent knees and arms flexed into pea-sized muscles. He grunted and walked around the room like King Kong.

She coughed to keep from laughing out loud.

"We're going to have to take the train to Boston leaving at three, so we should go after we eat," she said.

"I have always wanted to ride on a train. The tracks will shorten our trip," he said.

"Well, we would have arrived days ago if we had taken a plane."

"I am finished," he said, throwing his napkin down. He opened his suitcase and packed.

She wolfed down her dessert and half an hour later they checked out of the hotel.

They caught the subway at the Crystal City Station, got off at Union Station and walked to the Amtrak ticket window. She purchased two tickets to Boston's South Station. They had an hour and a half to wait for their train.

He sat on a bench, napping with his chin resting on his chest.

She sat beside him and squeezed her eyes shut, trying in vain to black out images of skeletons languishing in dusty storerooms. She still did not consider the Pecos skeletons family, but pitied their callous treatment at the hands of Kidder, who though moved by their humanity saw them as artifacts to enrich the knowledge of the scientific community and further his career. After he found the bones, he became consumed with death. He discovered at Pecos the same wealth the Spanish found, the Indians themselves. So many skeletons to unearth, not enough bones to satisfy him; not until he unburied every skeleton he could find and applied his stratigraphy techniques to the eldest layer buried beneath the rubbish. He grew quite adept at sifting through trash and finding priceless ivory. He boasted in his September entry that he dug up hundreds in the main plaza, beneath garbage piles, underneath floors, and in the center of the church, in the mass graveyard that was once Pecos Pueblo; he even found several priests. If the weather had not grown so cold, he would have dug up every Pecos who ever lived.

Kidder dug at Pecos 51 years after the Sand Creek Massacre, fishing on a scientific expedition, unlike crude soldiers piling chopped-off heads for an archaic Surgeon General. Technology had advanced and Kidder probably assigned numbers and placed a tag on each skeletal big toe.

I'm glad they were all taken together to the Peabody Museum; else they might have ended up scattered all over the place with no easy way to identify them. At least they've had each other for company. Grandfather would say she was getting sentimental about the bones, but she was just being human.

She opened the leather case, fished out a photo and examined the picture. Kidder sat surrounded by Pecos skeletons and a few caskets containing Spanish priests, four cardboard coffins, resembling the ones at the Smithsonian. Within each lay a skeleton dressed in a Franciscan's robe, looking rather monkish. The hoods of the friars were empty because the skeletons were headless. Black holes filled the place where their faces should have been. The skulls were tucked beneath the armpits of their robes. Obviously, the friars lost their heads over the Indians, just like Kidder did.

One skeleton wore spectacles. His eye sockets stared from a coffin that had the words, Agent of the Inquisition, scribbled on the side. Fray Bernal, the snakelike Franciscan of her nightmare.

She opened the diary and read silently.

October 22, 1915

We will leave soon, before the first snowfall. Frankly, I jump with joy to leave here and go back East to civilization. Piles of bones we've unearthed so far are a distance away from my tent but I swear I heard a skeleton rattle just now, perhaps my own. My appetite is poor of late and I've had to poke another hole in my belt. Can hardly wait to get back to Boston and eat a square meal. I am tired of green chili stew, pinto beans, Indian fry bread and corn. I haven't had a juicy steak in so long I can hardly remember the taste.

October 25, 1915

When I entered my tent, my servant fell to his knees. He opened his cupped hands and within laid the feathers of my prized roadrunner. He claims a rattlesnake entered my tent and swallowed my bird. He insists we return the Pecos bones to their graves. He claims Masawkat-sina sent the rattlesnake. My bird is a warning to rebury the bones and leave the holy burial grounds in peace. The man then scared the wits out of me. "Look, a ghost," he screamed.

I swung my head around to the same rattling noise of last night. I shook my servant until his teeth rattled. All along this varmint has been trying to scare me. I ordered him to go back to Grants. This man sabotaged me all along ever since he found out we are not just digging up the bones for examination and then reburial, but are taking them with us when we leave. I'm beside myself with grief over my bird. I had hoped to take my roadrunner back East and put him on display. It took quite a bit of trouble for my crew to trap the roadrunner with field-mice bait. Tomorrow, we load the trucks.

October 27, 1915

Last night, we found the man I fired a few miles from here near the Pecos River. His skin dried up like a human piece of jerky. I am sorry for my harshness with him. I tremble with guilt because I demanded he leave in the dead of night. Then I take another whiskey drink, steady my hands, and feel I did the right thing. An uneducated, superstitious Indian like him might have cut my throat while I slept; his eyes were so crazed. He believed in this Keeper of the Dead business and the bones being alive.

This afternoon, Jack ran into my tent, claiming he saw a ghost decked out in feathers climb from the hidden kiva. The ghost chased him with an ax.

I heard a ruckus outside, figured my dead servant's family paying me a visit, but then I don't know how his relatives would find out this quickly about his being fired. I picked up my gun and took a look see.

I opened the tent and Jack stood there, looking like a cantaloupe was caught in his throat. I smacked him on the back and told him to whip into shape because it's just the sun that's got him. We're all edgy. But then Jack clutched his chest, fell forward and hit the dust. I yelled for a doctor, but was too late. Jack either died from a heart attack or suffocation.

'What should we do with him?' I whispered. I shuddered yet tried to act strong in front of my team but Jack, with his tongue rolled back into his throat, looked monstrous; his eyes bugged out of his head. I clutched my stomach to keep from losing my lunch.

'We'll have to bury Jack at Pecos. His body will soon decompose,' Jim said.

The hardest thing I ever did, planting Jack at Pecos but Jim's right. This accursed sun is so hot, even at October's end, yet the nights are so cold. The only thing we can do is leave Jack behind. We hammered a piece of wood with his name carved on it. Jack wasn't religious. He was a man of science.

I asked Martin to write Jack's mother and tell her.

November 6, 1915

None of our vehicles will start. The mechanic's gone into Santa Fe for parts. This accursed sun and freezing nights have taken their toll on not only us but our transportation. It's snowing. The bones are loaded into the trucks, raring to brave the icy roads. The trucks barely had room for all the skeletons. Afraid some of the fellows and ladies broke. Itching to get back to civilization and leave the ruins behind.

Tonight I heard my tent flapping about. I complained to Jim about the wind but he swore the air was still. I've placed a guard outside my tent.

November 8, 1915

The vehicles are fixed but we've had another funeral, a freak accident. A driver stepped on the gas; the truck shot backwards and ran over Martin. How gruesome; the tires cut his body in half. The driver swears he set the gear to drive forward.

I've fired the mechanic against Jim's advice. Jim's shaken up about this Ruler of the Underworld business. I took him by the shoulders and told him snap out of it; Kachina magic is mere superstition. I reminded him other digs have had accidents before and other archaeologists killed in the line of duty, and weren't we lucky all these months nothing happened until now? We're all jittery after living in this godforsaken land for so many months with all the priests murdered here and the holy church burned to the ground. Maybe the underworld really is situated beneath the kivas and all this time we've been standing above hell.

I've booked us on the train for Boston leaving Santa Fe midmorning. I've ordered my driver to stand by. I intend to stay awake all night with the lantern burning. Jim's here with me; he doesn't want to sleep in his own tent.

And that was his last entry.

She stuffed the diary in the leather case with jerky movements but held onto the photo. In the picture, some distance behind Kidder, was a pile of skeletons. The bones were unwilling immigrants, transported from another time, another world.

She yawned and stretched. Nothing like a good read to relax.

Brr, she covered Grandfather with his blanket then wrapped her chest with a sweater, inhaling vanilla fabric softener.

She brooded at the photo of Kidder and the skeletons. Her head grew heavy and she nodded off.

She jerked up, thinking herself back in the campground at Cherry Creek.

She pushed the toe of her tennis shoe against the ashes of a dead fire.

Old-fashioned dusty tents and turn-of-the-century camping gear were scattered about the area.

The largest tent from which a light glowed beckoned her like a desert beetle to a bulb. The tent was filled with rusted archaeological stuff. She waved her hands at cobwebs that crisscrossed the tent opening.

Groping on her hands and knees, she poked her head further in. More copper-colored dirt covered a few ancient instruments. A cot was at the furthest end from her along with a stone bathtub-looking thingy with faded scratches that looked like odd writing, almost like hieroglyphics. A cluttered desk dominated the center of the tent. A soap box, turned upside down, was in front of the desk. The soap box was dusty, except for the imprint of a man's rear-end.

An Indiana-Jones style hat lay on the middle of the makeshift desk. The owner must have recently removed the hat from his head because fresh sweat soaked into the band. The tent was saturated with men's cologne intermixed with sweaty underarms, arrogance, and enough of a recklessness to make her shudder.

A black spider spun its way down a web from the ceiling to atop the hat. The spider had enormous pupils. The spider hopped to the edge of the hat and snapped its fangs at her.

She yanked her head back and shuddered at the spider.

Someone caught her sneaking out.

She stretched her neck and looked up at Alfred V. Kidder.

He was not impressed by her. He shoved her aside, spun on his heel and barked out orders.

Men ran bustling from tents, scurrying around the camp like prairie dogs.

They dug at fast speed, and made her dizzy from chattering that spun her ears like rewinding tape.

Ka-choo! Flying dirt made her sneeze.

Men shouted and dug, and packed and dug, and dug some more. They threw baskets in the air, carefully handled pottery bowls, wooden rosary beads, smashed Kachina pieces, and whatever other antiquities they unearthed.

Finally, they struck ivory.

Kidder strutted about a circle of oohing and aahing men. In his arms he swung a skeleton with long black hair hanging from its skull. A tag hung from its toe with the number one scribbled in bold black. The skeleton slung a bony arm across Kidder's back. A dull-looking turquoise ring circled the index finger bone of its skeletal hand.

A man walked over to Kidder and yanked the ring off the finger.

The skeleton's skull cocked at Kidder and appeared to grin at him with its big teeth.

Thunder cracked.

Lightning flashed.

Everyone looked up at the sky.

The skeleton turned its skull and gripped Kidder's jacket so that the fabric rumpled at his shoulder.

When the lightning show ended, no one but her seemed to notice the skeleton had moved. The skeleton stared at a tree, the bones on its face drooping and its eye sockets flattening to its cheekbones. There at the base of the tree, a moccasin peeked out.

She tiptoed over from the other side of the tree and sneaked up on the spy.

He may have been a thirteen-year-old boy instead of a ninety-eight-year-old man, but his eyes were just as passionate as the old man who slept in her camper.

She stood silently behind Grandfather, not wishing to embarrass him. On his face was such anguish. She didn't feel any special connection to the skeletons the grave robbers took, but the thought of anyone digging him up and shipping his bones to who-knows-where devastated her.

The archaeology crew loaded the trucks, circa 1915 with skinny tires, unlike modern delivery trucks with monstrous sixteen wheels. The truck sides were partially open, and reminded her of chuck wagons, allowing a driver to transport more inventory because items could stick out from the sides. The trucks were about the size of today's minivan.

Strangers bent to their knees and lifted the skeletons into their arms. It seemed their bony hands clung to the earth in protest or perhaps grasped a chunk of homeland, red dust dripping from bony fingers.

Men carried the skeletons to the trucks but their dry, brittle skulls could not cry out; their mouths opened in a silent scream.

The crew tossed the bones into the trucks: men, women, and children, some of them crunching. A few skeletons broke.

Skeleton piles in the trucks grew higher until the drivers climbed behind the wheels and their colleagues smiled from passenger seats.

Others climbed into cars, the archaeologist sitting real important-like in the biggest car, puffing on a cigar, and flecking the ashes at the red earth.

Others stayed behind, to clean up the camp, she supposed.

The engines roared to life and tires rolled across the dirt road, stirring up dust like a bull in a ring.

Bones stuck out the open truck sides. There was a crunch and a crack. No cushioning to protect the bony truck occupants.

Nineteen skulls peeked out the truck openings, looking towards Pecos with teeth bared and eye sockets longing for home.

Their bony arms reached out towards Grandfather, who had his own arms outstretched as he ran after the trucks.

"Governor," she yelled in a voice strangled with sobs but it seemed he could not see her.

She ran behind him and the distance, between them and the trucks, grew.

He lifted his head to the sky at a hawk and looked as though he wished he could turn into a bird and fly.

He ran harder, for miles.

He sickened from hunger and exertion, yet he chased after the bones.

His muscles weakened.

His head lightened.

His lungs collapsed.

His legs crippled, and he fell.

She lay beside him in the dust, both of them spread eagle, feeling the earth rumble, their heads grumble and their hearts tumble as they pushed their ears to the ground, hearing the roar of the trucks grow fainter.

He sat up and screamed.

Don't cry, she said but only mouthed the words. Even she couldn't hear herself speak.

He rose to his rocky feet and staggered in the middle of the road. Dust covered his face and mucus bubbled from his nose.

He stood alone. She was simply an observer who counted the wrinkles on his face and knew that at thirteen, he was the last surviving Pecos Indian. The look on his face made her afraid for him. Surely he wondered if he would end up the only one buried at Pecos.

All alone, no other bones in the ground to keep him company.

With rounded shoulders, he slugged back to the pueblo.

She followed and when he returned, he stumbled upon a leather case leaning against a wall of the church ruins.

He leafed through the diary with a desperate look on his face, unable to read Kidder's words, no clue where the bones had gone.

She awoke from her dream, sobbing quietly at the phobia on Grandfather's face that they would come for him, too.

Eskimos died and an anthropologist impatiently boiled the flesh from their bones.

Grandfather still snored beside her on the bench at Union Station.

She hugged him as if she might soak his bones into her body.

18

Grandfather sat on the bench, sipping a cup of coffee. She tapped her shoe, waiting for the train due at any minute.

She closed her eyes, imagining a man at the Santa Fe Station standing on the platform dressed in sweat-soaked clothing of an archaeologist. His crew loaded the bones onto crowded freight cars and with his lips moving silently, he counted boxes of skeletons stuffed like sardines.

With one hand, he checked his pocket watch, and with his other hand he clutched the fingers of a little skeleton girl who grasped in her skeletal hand a doll that looked like it was dug from a landfill. He planned to give the child to his mother, an avid collector of dead children.

A ghost train screeched to a halt on the tracks.

Workmen scuttled about carrying coffin-shaped acid-free boxes on their shoulders and loading them into windowless train cars.

The freight cars' metal doors slammed shut.

Locks snapped into place.

Kidder dragged the kidnapped child onto the train, patting her skull and holding her bones close to his waist.

The train moved, rolling along the tracks with skeletons crunching and shaken, rattling in fear along thousands of miles, the dark not comforting like their graves, and the train chugged further away from Pecos.

"The train's here," Grandfather said, jolting her out of imagining.

"How exciting, we'll arrive in Boston less than seven hours from now and tomorrow..."

"Yes," he said, interrupting her. His voice sounded flat and his eyes looked hollow. He peered down the length of the station.

"Don't worry so. I've arranged for your mattress to follow on a freight train. One more comfortable night and then you'll sleep on your rusty, smelly magic," she said.

He gave her a resigned look as she grasped his arm to board the train.

He sat by the window, looking out as if he didn't want to miss a thing.

The top of his head lined the window short enough so that they both could enjoy the passing scenery.

A dull ache twisted her heart at the thought of Steve. She concentrated instead on the rattling along the tracks. It seemed trains snaked across America through the ugliest parts of cities, garbage dumps, industrial wastelands.

The train rumbled along stopping occasionally, and at other times, bypassing platforms where people waited with biting nails.

They bought dinner from a trolley and he wolfed down two sandwiches, an apple, and a slice of chocolate cake, washing it all down with a bottle of water.

He leaned his chair back, let out a whopper of a burp, and was soon fast asleep.

She closed her eyes and soon dreamt she was back at the ruins and Grandfather a ten-year-old boy, burying his father. Graves surrounded him as he wandered amongst his dead relations with ghosts and skeletons walking alongside him, twisting their hands and beating their chests.

The winds flattened the mounds of graves.

Sunsets and clouds swirled around, moving time forward. He returned to the ruins, appearing to have grown a few inches, no longer a ten-year-old but a boy on the verge of his teen years.

The rocks he placed to mark the graves of his family vanished. Men scurried about with shovels, digging at the ruins and searching for archaeological treasures.

Grandfather ran in circles, dropping to his knees now and then and using his hands to dig. "Where are they? Where did I bury them?"

The train chugged across the tracks and jiggled her awake, her heart flopping about.

Beside her on the train seat, he whimpered, his face scrunched in pain.

She squeezed his hand and leaned his head across her chest.

"Sh. It's alright, Governor. I have been dreaming and you have shared my dream, and lived your sadness again."

"Granddaughter, my tongue has never been good with words, but I swear I have always done my best by you. I wish I had done more."

"You worked so hard all your life to feed me, to put clothes on my back, to shelter me, to try to keep me healthy. What else could you have done?"

"I might have treated you like a beloved granddaughter. We could have picked flowers from yellow fields of the sun. I ought to have laughed with you under the stars as we danced by the rays of the moon. I should have looked at you as a grandson and dragged you into the kiva to share the secrets of the Kachinas."

"Sh. It's okay. I understand."

"I would have kept you with me if worry had not ruled me. You were delicate, and I feared to break you so I placed you with the nuns like a bull in a pottery shop."

"Yes, Sister Catherine would have agreed with your description of me," she said, yawning.

"I had a distant uncle going way back, a carpenter by the name of Agustín Guichí. You get your stupidity from him I think."

"I'm not stupid," she said.

"It's a matter of interpretation, to use your words," he said, shrugging his shoulders. "Some say the beginning of the end for our pueblo actually occurred in 1760 when Bishop Tamarón, head of the Jesuits, blessed Pecos with a visit. The priests actually filed a lawsuit against the Franciscans to control New Mexico," he said, laughing, "And the bishop was trying to muscle in."

"I'm not stupid like great-great-whatever Uncle Agustín," she repeated, narrowing her eyes.

"Believe what you wish. Anyway, after the bishop's visit, Agustín and two friends rode in on asses, masquerading as Bishop Tamarón and his assistants. They wore makeshift costumes and in a three-day mockery Pecos held fiestas poking fun at the church. It was all in jest and after hearing confessions and dispensing tortilla bits of Holy Communion; Agustín went to work in his fields. A bear mauled him but ignored the corn, very odd since a bear never turns its back on food.

The bear pranced back up the mountain and was Catholic because he only wished to kill Agustín for his blasphemous mimicry. The Catholic god has no sense of humor, unlike our sacred Kachina clowns."

"So, like I've always said, Montezuma and the god of the Spanish, both punished Pecos. It seems we come from godless people," she said, aiming to hurt him as he hurt her.

"It's true God has no love for us," he said, making her instantly regret her words.

He stared out the window at the passing scenery. "Twenty-one years after Agustín died, the god of Moses sent a plague of locusts called smallpox that swept across all the pueblos, killing a fourth of the population, some five thousand souls. Pecos Pueblo was so poor by then, Charles III excused them from having to pay the Spanish war tax to help the Americans win their Revolutionary War," he said in a voice so soft she barely heard him.

He turned to her and lifted her chin, locking his eyes with hers. "I am as poor as a pueblo mouse. I only have the bones to give you at my death but remember that a man of science so valued these bones that he stole them. Don't ever forget the Spanish mined the Pecos Indians as if our pueblo was one of the Seven Cities of Cibola—in these bones we travel to bring home are pots of gold. For there is no value one can place on family and a man's soul and in these bones lives 2,067 souls."

"What you leave to me is priceless, Governor. Don't forget the ceremonial staff."

"I also leave you the pride of a majestic people so always hold your head up high and walk in the clouds."

"I will," she said.

Her head rolled around her shoulders and she swore not to fall asleep.

The grinding of the brakes jerked her awake. Just like the Pecos skeletons, she felt shaken and rattled as the train headed it seemed for a collision with Boston.

She rubbed her eyes, feeling groggy and disoriented. She squinted at the window and got her first view of the city that sparked the American Revolution, all over a spilled cup of tea. The Jemez Pueblo would have appeared like an ancient mud-hut world to a blueblood Bostonian descendant. Hell, her family was so poor a king wrote a note, excusing them from helping the U.S. gain its freedom. Some people who populate Massachusetts believe their ancestors, who settled in 1630, were the first Americans. She descended from Americans going back to the year 1100 and beyond. While Bostonians could boast about graves dating from the Seventeenth Century, she visited to claim her ancestors' bones, some from the Fifteenth Century.

"Wake up. We're here, Governor," she whispered in his ear, shaking his shoulder.

He moved as limp as a rag doll.

Ah, he wet his pants.

She shook him again to awaken him but somewhere on the tracks to Boston, he died in her arms, not alone this time, not so misunderstood. She did not know where he died nor at what time. Were they still at Philadelphia then? Had they passed New York or had they crossed the state line of Rhode Island? She could never say Grandfather died at Delaware, or Grandfather passed in New Jersey.

But...he was really dead. The reflection of the train window showed skeletons form in the Pecos dirt, like in her dream, rise up to greet him and suck him back into the dust with them, leaving a vision of herself, alone in the middle of the ruins with her face covered by dust, the last surviving Pecos.

No. Oh, no.

She wailed, rocking, with him in her arms.

"Wake up. Don't leave me all alone, so alone, forever alone."

The men in white jackets came for him then, because she was so loud.

They wanted to take him away but she clung to him and fought them, kicking at the seats.

Finally, they both got off the train, her dragged by her armpits and him on a stretcher.

"Wait. I don't want him to be cold," she said.

She pleaded with them to stop so she could cover him. She would be nice. She wouldn't try to scratch or bite, promise.

She covered him with his blanket.

"To warm you with my love," she whispered and stroked his withered chest.

He stared back with lifeless eyes.

With shaky fingers, she placed his blanket over his face.

"Here, this fell from his pocket," an attendant said, handing her a note with her name on it. He gave her a card and told her when to come see about the arrangements.

She nodded her head, dazed.

Another attendant led her to the women's bathroom.

She slammed a stall door, sat down and unfolded the note which read: Granddaughter, my friend Jerry Norberto, writes this for me as I tell him what to say. You are an old fool's joy, yet I have been harsh with you. I leave you the pride of the Pecos people.

She tapped the ceremonial staff against the ground.

With a trembling chin, she read his last words he would ever convey to her.

Walk with your head in the sun, for you are a queen now, and have always been my princess.

She lost it then, crying so hard she almost passed out. She swore her tears would never stop flowing. He had loved her and she was too stupid to realize it so she hid her own love. Now it was too late.

She crawled out of the stall, and used the sink for support so she could pull herself up, huffing and puffing because her heart weighed a ton.

She ran the water and shoved her face beneath the faucet.

Her image in the mirror was of a shrunken, Native American woman, hair dripping wet, not dressed warm enough for a cool Boston evening, thin shoulders shivering, clutching a letter soaked with tears. Her face appeared terrified and her mouth opened in a silent scream. Ever since she saw skeletons at the Smithsonian, pity for the Pecos bones squeezed her chest.

I promise. Whatever it takes, I promise. His wish was for me to bring the bones home. They are after all...my family, but thoughts of ancient bones stir no love in my heart. My family is the old man lying at a morgue in Boston. I care for no other bones but his.

She tried to dial her cell phone but the numbers were so small and her fingers shook, so she dragged her shoes through the bathroom exit to a pay phone and by the ninth try, dialed correctly and reached Steve.

"He's dead. Oh, Steve, Grandfather's left me for good. What am I to do now? How will I live?"

"You'll survive, Holly, just like you always have."

"Come quick. I need you."

She hung up the phone, and slid down the glass wall of the phone booth.

She didn't know how long she sat like that at the train station, looking out the windows at the fading light.

19

The bouncing taxi reminded her of her pickup, when she rode to Pecos with Grandfather joggling in the back on his mattress. She looked back, expecting to see his ghost. There was one more Pecos ghost, a living ghost, herself. Since his death, a voice nagged at her that if she understood the bones more, then she would understand him, and perhaps find peace herself. However, her family roots were a bitter herb to swallow because he died without realizing his dream. It was impossible to believe him dead. She kept peering at the seat next to her, expecting to see him puffing away at a hand-rolled cigarette, his crappy hat jauntily on his head.

Oh, Governor, I miss you so.

She slammed the door of her hotel room and kicked off her shoes.

She held her head in her hands and rocked, on the sofa. She grieved alone, a zillion miles from home in what seemed like a foreign country, the Eastern U.S., Boston, big city, bright lights, tea and snobbery. She landed in Boston like a half-dead fish drowning in the Pecos River. She longed to call Steve but he had to get up at three a.m. and drive to Albuquerque to catch his flight.

Grandfather would roll over at the morgue if he knew she shoved the ceremonial staff against the door handle to prevent any intruders from breaking in.

She lumbered to the bedroom and changed into sweats, peeling her clothes off and letting the garments fall. She shuffled into the bathroom and brushed her teeth then gulped down a pain pill, hoping the drug would knock her out like a sledge hammer.

She heard a jingle, spun around, and gasped at Grandfather who stared back at her from the mirror. He was dressed in the old way with leather shirt and breastplate shield made from bones. His only nod to the modern was a black, round felt hat on his small head. His hat brim reached the tip of his white bushy brows. A crushed feather stuck out from the hat band. He appeared shrunken, his hands nearly reaching his knees, yet a presence about him made him appear tall because a light glowed from him. White hair swirled around his face.

She spun around.

There was no one behind her. Just like him to play tricks.

She turned back around and he stared at her from the mirror. Grandfather, she mouthed to his image.

He held a cupped hand to her, as if offering something.

She touched the mirror but her fingers banged against cold glass.

Had he come for her, like in movies where a loved one crosses over to lead the way? Maybe her time had come, perhaps not. She had not completed her quest to take the bones home to Pecos.

It was not so shocking that the old man was here, near his death place, where perhaps the other world lay just beyond.

He had haunting grey eyes, like so many elderly have, because life has begun to fade from their sight as the curtain of death slowly closes. One has to merely pull the cord to cross over to the other side.

His expression was sad...so sad...slowly...he faded from the mirror.

"Don't leave me. Please help me," she said tearfully, knowing that if she looked behind, he would not be there. Her heart twisted as her loss swept over her, like a tsunami. She swayed and rubbed her eyes. What does this vision mean?

She thumped her chest with her fist, and a hollow sound vibrated her ribcage. Her heart had been missing for years. Perhaps he was right and when the bones were reburied at Pecos, she would dig out her own heart. She would become a better person, a good wife, and maybe even a mother. Perhaps life would flow within and fill up her hollowness which only grew deeper in the last few hours.

A clattering noise vibrated in the sink, sounding like pebbles falling.

Peyote buttons rolled down the sides and settled at the drain.

The sink had been empty except for a few water drops from washing her hands.

She picked up the buttons and wiped her damp cheeks with the backs of her hands. Even in death he had magic. He left her the peyote, just what she craved. Peyote would erase her pain, if only for a while. She, too, belonged to the Native American Church and believed in both Christian theology and the ancient Peyote Religion. The Peyote sacrament substituted as the Catholic host to commune with God without the hindrance of a priest. The hallucinatory drug filled her with a sense of well-being and acted medicinal.

The midnight bell tolled. Luckily, she skipped dinner. Only an idiot swallowed peyote on a full stomach.

She dragged each button across the desk and blew on the hairy tufts then scraped the hair away with a butter knife before stuffing each button into her mouth and chewing. As bitter-tasting peyote seeped into her cheeks and down her throat, she imagined creamy butter on a light croissant. She chewed until her jaw grew sore, until the peyote turned to juice else her stomach would have hurled; peyote had such a nasty taste. There now, almost over. Swallow the last button.

Rubbing her forehead against the desk, she clutched her stomach and breathed deeply. Don't throw up. Think of something else, like pinto beans. Green chile stew. Indian tacos with cheese, crispy lettuce and juicy tomatoes. Yum-yum. Yuck. What a foul taste.

Oh, God, I miss Grandfather so much.

She rolled her chin around the wooden desktop and her bones cracked. Damned tension knotted her muscles. The clock ticked loud, making her dread the first hour of wanting to vomit and die. These and other discomforts were worth it though because eight hours of blissful hallucination would follow her initial reaction.

Ah. An hour's gone by.

She ran a hand through her sweat-soaked hair and massaged her temples. It felt like a bowling ball balanced on her neck and a dull ache throbbed at the base. The room twirled and wiggled and she didn't dare lift her head else she would fall from the chair. She gripped the arms. Okay, there is nothing wrong with your heart. Palpitations are normal.

Good...finally...the taste and smell of peppermint, one of those Life Savers, the white ones. Or the green candies? Little green hole in the center...

Her skin froze like those times in the damp kiva of her nightmares, cold like a grave.

She rubbed her arms and shivered. Her heart had a hole because he died.

On her bedroom dresser at home was a photo of an old man holding a little girl in his arms, her hands pinching his cheeks and making a face at him. The old man laughed and his eyes twinkled. Why were there such few happy memories except for a couple of old photos?

The room whirled and light faded to black.

She tumbled into a dark hole, only a caterpillar smoking on a mushroom did not lead her astray.

She clutched the chair so tightly her finger may have broken.

Don't let go of the goddamned chair. Don't. If you let go of the chair, you will fall into Shipapu where Masawkatsina awaits.

The Keeper of the Dead knew her. She would not escape him this time.

Quick! Run and hide. Don't let Masawkatsina find you.

Hold tight. If I fall, my head will crack open on the floor, only I won't blossom in the crack that now had yellow flowers growing from the tile.

What happens to the sunflower, come the cold grey winter? The sunflower dies…

The hair rose at the back of her neck because the door creaked open.

Something crawled on its hands and knees, waddled between the legs of her chair, and lifted her up…

It wanted to kill her. If she fell from the chair she would die.

She hiccupped and clutched the chair tighter.

Why did the clock stop? What…? Oh God. Don't look. Keep your eyes closed. Think. Think. Concentrate on something else. What…?

Oh, yeah, Life Savers. Those beautiful white…wafers? Candy? Or mint green? A pungent green like the pine trees of Pecos. What did he say about bloody trees? Already, her memories faded. Oh, God, one day she wouldn't even remember his face.

Slowly, painfully, time passed and her chair lowered, floating back to the floor.

Once again the clock ticked but the hand moving sounded like a loud knock on the door.

Don't let it in.

She lifted her heavy head and observed the clock numbers. The numbers of both hands looked fuzzy, like when an eye doctor splashes those funny drops in her eyes.

An intense face in a white jacket, wearing spectacles, bent over her. He held an eye dropper over her face and nearly poked her eyeballs.

Liquid swirling around her eyeballs didn't help her vision.

Slowly, the man faded from view.

She blinked at an eye chart on the wall. Uh...E D F C Z P... twenty-twenty...

Her head rolled around her neck and the fridge swelled. The counter tops rolled like an ocean wave.

She saw with a cat's night vision, or might see this clearly if roaring drunk. The hallucination of peyote always made her feel like she could see through walls.

A bee buzzed in her ear and left a drop of fresh honey on her tongue.

The aroma of baked bread slammed against her nostrils and Old-Woman shoved a piece of bread in her mouth. The odor of legumes, grown as a family staple for centuries, had a homey smell and she clung to Old-Woman, begging her not to leave.

But Old-Woman faded away and left her holding a piece of air.

Paint on the kitchen walls peeled and exposed a layer of sun-baked adobe.

Fresh earth dirtied her nostrils.

She was home, this room no longer a modern kitchenette but the walls freshly packed into baked mud.

Clean ceramic dishes on the counter top petrified into wooden dishes.

A group of Native Americans materialized from the adobe walls. Each held a wooden bowl and spoon. These Indians who smiled at her, dressed like the ancients and appearing old-fashioned, were strangers.

She cocked her ear to the bedroom. No dream catcher spinning. She did hear whisperings, but the gurgle of excited voices did not come from the bedroom. Ah, blessed peyote brought her this living dream and these visitors.

Guttural sounds came from the people who danced in her kitchen. There were ninety-six men and one hundred women, some old, some young, and a few hundred or so children of various ages all chattering in Towa.

They spoke...to her, held their arms out...to her, smiled...at her.

Rise to you feet. Greet them. Oak scraped against tile.

Happy faces smiled and beckoned with a finger to come closer.

She floated on air towards the gathering, shyly looking down at the dirt floor. Reddish dust stirred on her tennis shoes.

The others, the ones who pointed at her and flirted with her, wore moccasins on their feet. The dust of Shipapu stirred around their ankles.

"Welcome," each person whispered to her.

One stroked her cheek. Another touched her arm. Others brushed her face with soft lips. The smell of the Pecos River rose from the roots of black hair, grey hair, and white hair.

"I am your Auntie," one whispered.

"I am an uncle," another said.

"I am your cousin," a young woman said, smiling and squeezing her hand.

The gathering separated and one-by-one, each pointed to a cradle in the corner.

She walked towards the cradle half-covered by a colorful ceremonial rug. There had been a birth in this room. Gifts for the baby lay on the floor beside the cradle; one was a rattle created from two rattlesnake tails. As a child, she had such a rattle left over from infancy, a gift from him.

"You are of the Snake Clan," they all chanted.

She held back her tears and looked down at the cradle, fearing the worst.

Ah, a live child.

An infant girl with an adult face squinted at her. It was like looking into a mirror at her reflection.

Fingers touched her hair.

Warm breath caressed her neck and blew into her ears.

"How we have missed you, Child. We have always loved you. In your heart you have known us."

She squeezed her eyes and her damp lashes brushed her cheek.

A loud rattle, many loud rattles, jingled around her, but the snake rattle lay still. Instead of flesh and blood family, a gathering of skeletons balanced on their bony feet. Child skeletons wrapped bony arms around bony legs of adult skeletons. One child skeleton balanced atop an adult's shoulders. Other children with small skeletal hands clutched adult hands.

The skeletons rocked, on feet of brittle bones.

No. Oh, no. Please.

Their eye sockets emptied of every remnant of life.

The skeletons collapsed to the dirt floor with a crashing sound.

Red dust swirled around the bones until they vanished.

She leaned against the adobe wall and sat hunched over, breathing deeply. The cracks in her heart were bigger than the cracks in this surreal kitchen's adobe.

She dropped to her knees and covered her face with her hands. Usually peyote made her feel giddy and light and...A familiar pain slammed against her chest and closed up her bleeding hole, like a hot poker cauterizing her wound. He was gone and never coming back.

An electrifying noise vibrated the walls; and the kitchen vanished; and Grandfather's shed faded in.

She tiptoed to the shed window and peeked in but the dilapidated building was deserted except for a hooting owl perched on a rickety chair, an eagle walking about the room like it was pigeon-toed, and a table saw roaring at high speed. The table saw was wishful thinking. Impoverished Grandfather could not purchase what he considered a high-tech saw, nor did his shed ever have electricity.

She kicked in the door of the shed and chased out the birds with a broom used to sweep sawdust from the floor. The table saw followed, running on its four legs.

A ratty table held a jar of nails, hammer, and enough dirt to build a child's play pueblo. A few stray hand-tools hung from the wall, a wrench, saw, a screwdriver. Two-by-fours were scattered about. Remnants from his latest masterpiece, leftovers when he made her dream catcher, littered the floor.

She waved the broom around her head, knocking tools down from the wall and creating havoc for spiders that spun webs from the ceiling. Jars filled with nails and screws, Grandfather's filing system, fell from shelves shattering glass everywhere. One jagged piece struck her in the heart but the pain still wasn't enough so she took the broom and beat the table until her arms hurt so badly she couldn't lift them.

Still, the splintery table stood magic-like, hard as steel and just as unfeeling.

She dropped the broom to the floor, nothing but toothpicks now. Her arms hung from their sockets, nothing but a rag doll. The last time she felt this excruciating pain was when the train pulled into Boston and he left her all alone, so alone, like now.

The whistle of a train blared from the walls and fog filled up the shed with smoke.

When the fog cleared, a door slid open and Grandfather exited the train. He tapped his high-top tennis shoe, all decked out in a black tuxedo with tails and top hat to boot, with an ostrich feather sticking out of a red hat band and eagle feathers woven through his braids.

20

A light in the shed glowed brighter, until a chandelier shone on her head, illuminating her. She no longer wore sweats but a black, flowing ball gown.

At one end of the shed, a transparent orchestra tuned their violins and cellos. They all wore Kachina masks, leather skirts and moccasins that brushed their knees. One musician floated in the air, banging on piano keys, though no piano existed.

Grandfather bowed at the waist. "I believe we never danced at your wedding," he said, taking her hand and leading her to the dance floor covered with sawdust.

"As I recall, you waltzed with a wine bottle and toasted your friends," she said, giving him a curtsy.

"Ah, the rosé has always been the maid of honor," he said, smacking his lips.

He reached out and pulled the glass piece from her chest. He wore gold silk armed with diamond cuff links. He glared at the bloody shard of glass in his hand. "Did you save a piece of your heart, so it can grow whole again?"

"Oh, Governor," she said, flinging herself into his arms, those silk arms that felt so strong.

He ran his hand down her hair and stroked her like a wounded animal.

"You were right when you told me you would die soon," she said, hiccupping.

"It's a heavy burden, knowing everything; I have a Pdh in life," he said.

"You mean PhD. Will you take me with you, when you leave?"

"It is not your time yet. You have barely even lived. Why would you want to miss the rest of your life, Child?"

"I don't know," she said, shrugging her shoulders.

"Always remember that you did not hurry my death. My coming to Boston with you did not kill me. Now, let's have some music," he roared.

The notes of a haunting waltz echoed from instruments of ghost Kachinas.

He placed an arm around her waist and swirled his other hand from behind his back, taking her hand in his.

They twirled around the room, circling a ten-foot wedding cake.

Around and around they turned in that dusty shed with nails vibrating from the floor.

"This is why I have come to see you. I did not ask Masawkatsina to allow me this visit to talk of death. I came to dance with my best girl."

"I bet all those women corpses are jealous, huh?"

"All my wives and mistresses are fighting over me."

When the song finished, he bowed and handed her the yellow rose from his button hole.

"I see you picked flowers from the yellow fields of the sun," she said.

"And I see you take your dancing after me. I was always best at Kachina dances," he said.

She curtsied back and smiled.

"Again," he roared.

Music filled the room and he snapped his fingers so that the roof vanished, replaced with what seemed like a million stars overhead.

He spun her around, and the moon's rays glowed silver on the dance floor.

"I always wanted to dance with you," he said.

"I thought you could only dance Kachina-style to the drums of the gods," she said.

"For you, I have taken lessons," he said, laughing. "See. My time has not been wasted since I rode into Boston, like a big shot, on a train."

"I always wanted to dance with you, Governor," she said, smiling.

They danced in that surreal shed, until sawdust came together and her heart was wood once more.

They danced until the effects of peyote wore off.

They danced until she spun past the dresser mirror and the reflection of a woman, clothed in sweats, resting her hand on an invisible shoulder and her other hand clenching the air.

She stopped dancing and opened her clenched fist. A yellow rose with dewy petals, the magic of the old man. She lowered her lips to the flower and once more heard his voice that last day on the train: We could have picked flowers from yellow fields of the sun. I ought to have laughed with you under the stars as we danced by the rays of the moon.

She jumped into bed and yanked the covers to her chin. It was nearly nine a.m. and she frowned at her still dream catcher she had hung from the ceiling, hoping for a connection to the old man. The dream catcher turned slowly, not fast enough to conjure up a dream, just enough to stir whisperings in Towa. She listened for his voice but he wasn't there with the other ghosts.

Her heart splintered into toothpicks and she fought the urge to cry herself to sleep so she could rest until Steve came. His plane arrived around 2:00 this afternoon.

21

At the funeral home he lay on his mattress wearing ankle-length moccasins and a Kachina kilt made from the finest white leather that Steve brought from home. A bright red sash draped his bare chest.

He appeared waxy with his dead snake eyes following her while she prepared him for burial. His eyes refused to remain closed; just like him not to want to miss a thing.

She washed his arms, legs and chest with water from a sacred spring, then rubbed his limbs and chest with bright yellow cornmeal. She stuffed his hands with cornmeal and bent his fingers.

"So the gods may know your heart is pure," she said, placing a white feather plucked from a turkey breast in his fists.

"So the gods may know you are faithful," she said, adding beside each feather a prayer stick made from willow shoot.

"So the gods may know you are bound to them," she said, tying his hands together on his stomach with a string.

The lower half of his face she painted sky blue and the top half bright yellow. She glued around his face a circular headdress made from white feathers with yellow and black tips. The feathers represent sun rays and like the sun, he radiated strength to all who knew him. He was Kachina priest, the incarnate of Sun Kachina, who would recognize his kindred spirit and ease him over to the other side.

For now, he lay on a sheet of cotton balls, which would help him float to the sky and join the cloud people. Occasionally, he would return to sprinkle the earth with rain.

She washed his hair with wet yucca leaves, combed his white head and wrapped ornamental ties of turquoise beads around each braid. She dusted him with funeral herbs he brought with him to Boston. It was a Shaman's way to foresee his own death so, he knew he would never see the bones again but wanted to make this trip with her so that they might...ah, he knew he would leave her. He contrived to spend his last days with her. When he lay in his coma at the Santa Fe hospital, he must have pleaded with Masawkatsina to give him more time so that he might bond close to her.

Even he could not stop the curse that killed every Pecos, which is probably why sorcery drew him in the first place. His stubbornness to find a cure kept him alive for so long, and he had been determined to continue the Pecos line through her, but failed. He would be buried with the bones so they could all be together in the afterlife. He would be with his close relations and other ancestors.

"And with Mama and Daddy. You won't be alone anymore with just a sassy bitch to keep you company," she whispered.

She repaired the cornmeal on his chest, which her tears threatened to turn to mush.

Flowing over each shoulder, two braids brushed his stomach.

A wooden cross hung around his neck, "Because we believe in the resurrection of the spirit."

"So you can have a smoke with Pautiwa and the ancient ones," she said, balancing his ceremonial pipe between his tied hands.

"So you might soar even higher in death," she said, straightening his old hat best she could and placing it beneath his armpit.

She bent his knees so he could be buried sitting up with his medicine bundle in his lap.

She kissed his cold lips.

"Even in death, you taste like magic, Governor."

She tapped the ceremonial staff against the floor, her inheritance, along with the Pecos ruins, skeletons, and other cultural antiquities. Her inheritance consisted of priceless artifacts, yet she felt dirt poor.

Steve flung his arm around her shoulder and she nestled her nose in his chest.

"I wish to God that I had been nicer to him and more patient," she said.

"He knew you loved him, Holly. You put your life on hold and drove him here."

"Oh, Steve, my sun has set and will never rise again. I shall nevermore feel his strong rays."

"We'll see him again at sacred ceremonies when Sun Kachina climbs from the kiva to join us," he said.

She vowed to have faith and clung to Steve's arm, a little too tightly.

"Let's go get the bones," she said.

"You'll feel better then; it's what he wanted but first, you must smoke your body to drive out the evil spirits. I have brought some incense for just this purpose."

"He had no evil spirits," she said, jabbing him in the ribs with her elbow.

She walked with her head down and believed she would never feel better. She wanted to strike out and hit Steve but Grandfather would be angry with her. She made sure by the way he was dressed for burial, that he was the sun and the light through all eternity.

There was no more room for darkness.

She spun on her toes, ran back to Steve and kissed his cheek.

22

The five-story, red-brick Peabody Museum of Archaeology and Ethnology was located on Divinity Avenue so she expected some holy guidance, but so far all she got was lost. She clung to Steve as they climbed the steps to the third floor, looking for her meeting place with Harvard dignitaries.

"I don't see why archaeologists are invited. They only want to see me because they're curious about what a living Pecos Indian looks like," she said

"Don't worry so much. I won't let them put you under a magnifying glass."

"Don't say anything about Grandfather. Say you decided to come with me instead," she said, gripping his sleeve.

"Okay, but you're acting paranoid. I need to use the head," he said.

"I'll just browse until you return."

Dark glasses hid her red eyes and swollen lids. She wandered into the Encounters with the Americas Gallery which displayed native cultures of the Aztecs and Mayans and an Aztec glyph of Quetzalcoatl, the feathered serpent god of the Aztecs.

She moved on to a display encased behind glass.

Her reflection faded out and Grandfather's face faded in. He seemed to belong with Quetzalcoatl; his eyes slanted like snake eyes. He wore a shirt printed in the pattern of Ridge-nosed rattlesnake skin. He flicked his tongue at her.

She twisted around to his ghost.

He was dressed in white, glowing buckskin; his hair no longer braided or greasy but lustrous and waved around his head, as if someone held a fan behind him. He was transparent and did not seem out of place here with Aztec relics, a Pecos Indian in cowboy boots. They had their own feathered serpent and claims to Montezuma.

He balanced on snakeskin boots also with the markings of a Ridge-nose. His boots brushed his knees. To top off his head, a ten-gallon cowboy hat, with a turkey feather sticking from the brim, swept the ceiling. Giant snakes. Big birds. Shiny magic.

Be strong as a thunderstorm and elegant as lightning, his voice whispered in her ear, though he did not move, not even his lips.

She held out her hand. Ah. You died too soon. I wanted to ask you so many questions. There was so much left unsaid between us. I wanted to show you Boston and the big Atlantic waters. I longed to show you off, as we rode around the city in a carriage like royalty; you with your magic hat waving at the people and me with my arm around you. We could have pounded the carriage floor with the staff to announce our coming. I wished to have fish and chips with you and tea with our pinkies held out. I wanted to...

Thanks for the train ride, the smokes and the dance.

His ghost slowly faded from view until all that remained was a white feather, ostrich-size, lying on the floor.

She stroked her cheek with the feather, marveling at its softness until she no longer held a feather but the ceremonial staff that scratched her cheek. She almost tripped from the heaviness as she balanced the staff in her arms.

He once asked if he visited after death, would he terrify her. She was not frightened by his ghost but mad because he did not live to see the bones returned to Pecos.

She was an endangered species and her shoes echoed with a solitary hollowness as she walked over to the bathrooms where Steve waited.

"Let's do this," she said, gulping at the crowd drifting in.

They made their way over to the gathering, him leading her by the hand. She dug her fingernails into his palm as a sea of people shook her hand.

She stepped up to the podium, stared into space and in an unfeeling voice spoke about family, loss, and blood. She talked about the disappearance of a way of life when Hispanic towns popped up like ant hills and no one needed to trade at Pecos anymore. Then the Americans came, like Walmart, in their covered wagons filled with goods to sell at their desert flea markets, and trade on the Santa Fe Trail usurped their livelihood. Consequently, Pecos became a ghost town due to a dwindling population lost to disease of the white man, Comanche raids, drought and famine.

"The cathedral was destroyed during the Pueblo Revolt and then resurrected after the Spanish reconquest. By the time Harvard sent an archaeologist to scratch in the dirt, seeking my people, our culture, and our history, American settlers who came from the north and the east had stripped the church of its wooden beams and roof. All who wanted monumental pillars, and wood with ornamental carving mined the Pecos church of its architecture."

"Must you take the bones? Science will suffer," one archaeologist said.

"I promised my grandfather."

"But we are more than happy to give you the other items taken from Pecos, as required by NAGPRA. There are hundreds of jewelry pieces, ceramic pots, tools, even a decorated Spanish spur from the Sixteenth Century. However, the Pecos bones are the specimens that contributed to the medical community's work on landmark studies of osteoporosis, skull injuries, and even dental science."

"I am glad that the bones have not been idle but contributed to the health of mankind, but they are tired now and their work here is done. It is my responsibility, as the last of the Pecos, to take their bones home and rebury them, and my grandfather's dying wish. If he stood here with me now, he would tell you to dig up your own relatives and study their bones."

"But..."

"Do you have other bones to dissect?" she said.

"About 20,000 but because of NAGPRA we must repatriate 12,000. You're taking the largest collection of one society that has ever been exhumed anywhere. There is much we can still learn from the Pecos bones."

"My people conceive that once a person is buried, he or she must remain in their resting place, else their soul can never find peace. I do not blame the university or the archaeologist; it was the way of the world then and I'm sure Alfred Kidder meant no harm. In many ways, you acted as caretakers for my family; you have kept them together and for this, I thank you."

She nodded her head at the curator of the museum for him to lead her to the bones.

23

They followed the curator to a massive storage room. A ceiling light illuminated hundreds of boxes, a few open. Bones stuck out from one box on the floor. Other bones were scattered about. Whole skeletons lay strewn across the floor and on tables in straight lines.

"All of us at the museum can only imagine how you must feel to finally meet the bones of Pecos Pueblo. We'll give you some privacy," the curator said and bowed his head.

In some open boxes, skeletons were stuffed like sardines with bony arms and legs entangled. The elbow bone of one stuck into the eye socket of another.

Two skeletons hugged with their skulls cheek-bone-to-cheek-bone.

Other skeletons were broken in half, the hip of one jammed into the ribcage of another skeleton where once a heart beat.

Two other skulls touched in a lipless kiss.

The bony fingers of one skeleton bent into fists, and the tips of its finger bones dug into the palms of another's bones, as though grasping to hold hands.

Despite her vows to harden her heart, her chest filled up with marshmallows. All this time, she wrestled with visions of her ancestors and denied them but now, witnessing evidence of their ordeal, such love burned in her chest, she might melt from the emotion. Her shoulders shook with sobs so deep, her shoulder blades touched. She never expected to care so much, but skulls with sunken eye sockets, longing for home, stared up at her.

She could hear his voice as they stood that day at the ruins, surrounded by ghosts. Your family lived on this red earth since the year 1300. They were born here. They married here. They made love here. They died here.

Though many of these bones were far removed from her generation, here were the aunts, uncles, and cousins she always longed for, perhaps even her grandmother, great-grandparents, great-great-grandparents and beyond. During her peyote hallucination the visitors in her adobe kitchen had said to her: How we have missed you, Child. We have always loved you. In your heart you have known us.

Some of these skeletons were Franciscan friars killed during the revolt, the one with a large crucifix perhaps twenty-six-year-old Fray Pedrosa, the friar who stayed behind at the Pecos Convento while his superior, Velasco, fled and was ambushed by rebels before he could reach Galisteo.

Even the Catholic Church abandoned her people in 1782 when the Pecos mission was declared part of the mission of Santa Fe. Priests rarely visited after that, leaving the people without the sacraments and no spiritual leader to bury their dead. The missionaries abandoned the Lord's vineyard for more potent wine in rich Santa Fe.

Some skeletons were buried with possessions to take to the afterlife. One lay on the floor grasping a hoe in his skeletal fingers.

Nowhere were there adult skeletons hugging child skeletons since Kidder separated the mothers from their children.

From one box, a small skull peeked out with wide eye sockets.

"A child who wishes to play once more at Pecos," she whispered.

She picked up a ball made from worn buffalo hide, placing the ball, along with a child-size bow and arrow, into a box of little bones.

On the floor was the remains of a miniature Indian lodge village that must have busted; perhaps the parents upset at his death. She placed the pieces into a box that contained a skeleton, the size of a three-year-old.

Pecos children buried with their toys so they can play in the afterlife.

Were any who survived the trek to Jemez here in this room? He said the people always went back to their roots; even the ones born at Jemez were buried at Pecos.

Here is your family, his voice whispered in her ear.

His presence vibrated in this room; he had followed her from the Aztec and Mayan exhibits.

Steve touched her shoulder.

She turned to him and he hugged her, both of them laughing and crying at the same time.

The curator patted her on the back.

"How do you feel?" he said.

"Seeing my ancestors' bones is like what the Jews felt when seeing pictures of Nazi death camps and corpses unearthed from mass graves. Look how they've desecrated my people. I always believed Grandfather was my only blood family, but he was right. Here lays my family, these bones," she said, her voice breaking.

She knelt and scooped up a bit of reddish dust.

"This Pecos earth is my family. See. I am not alone after all," she said, smiling through her tears.

She pointed her arms at the boxes and addressed the bones in Towa.

She and Steve stood in a moment of silence with their heads bowed, holding their hands in prayer.

When she finished, she unclasped her hands and her arms hung limp at her side.

"What did you say?" the curator said.

She shook her head in the negative, too choked up to speak.

"Holly asked the bones if they wish to go home to Pecos. The bones all answered her with eagerness, 'Home is what we long for. Home is where fields of maize grow and ceremonial kivas are. Home is where the others wait for us'," Steve said.

"I love you," she whispered in Steve's ear.

He lifted her off the ground and swung her around.

24

Steve flew back to Albuquerque to finalize the burial arrangements. She wasn't taking any chances with her family and would accompany her ancestors on their journey home.

Her last night in Boston she lay blinking at the ceiling of her hotel room. Her heart beat with dread because her dream catcher spun counter-clockwise. She clenched the sheet with white knuckles. Tomorrow, the bones would leave the Peabody Museum and head back to the Pecos ruins. She fulfilled her promise. Why then did the dream catcher taunt her?

The Pecos Pueblo stretched before her. She lifted her hand to her forehead and squinted.

It was the crack of dawn. One Indian stood like a statue on the roof of a pueblo apartment with his eyes fixated on the east, like so many had done before him, waiting for Montezuma to return with the sun to Pecos.

Another man leaned against the wall and gazed listlessly back at her.

A lone dog barked and a scrawny chicken ran in circles.

Wagons rolled by the pueblo carrying settlers, trade goods and traveling priests.

None of the wagons stopped at the pueblo.

The few surviving Pecos Indians watched Spanish settlers build a village nearby and claim the surrounding land as their own, land that really belonged to them by royal decree. Just because land is vacant due to dwindling population, does not mean the land is not theirs.

The winds of time blew matted buffalo hides around the pueblo.

From the outskirts, a band of people staggered through the pueblo gates and into the outside world, blinking their eyes like ghosts imprisoned for a hundred and sixty-one years. Thirty Pecos Indians trudged across *their* trail of tears. With dull eyes and skin graying like the ashes of their pueblo, they carried few possessions. It was obvious from their haggard appearance that they were abandoning their home, once the mightiest and richest pueblo in New Mexico but now crumbling to ruins. They undertook their eighty-mile journey to the Jemez Pueblo, taking turns lugging their Patrona, a testimony to their faith. Their own trail of tears stretched before them, yet they chose to carry her wooden slab when they could have brought more wild berries with them. They appeared weak from hunger and would probably have to share the burden of carrying their patron saint. The strong supported the elderly and weak. Two women pulled a litter upon which a man moaned.

Hollow-Woman followed with a heart of stone, thinking it would take them at least three days to make their journey.

She looked back at the pueblo, remembering from her first dream how it looked in its heyday three centuries ago with 2,000 residents and 500 warriors looking down from the rooftops. Now, the roofs crumbled and in many buildings, walls caved in as if some god took a mighty fist and pounded the pueblo. The cathedral was the only building that stood tall and upright though it, too, showed signs of wear.

Her ancestors' acreage had dwindled since in the distance squatters' homes of Spanish settlers and their Pecos Village trespassed upon the land belonging to Pecos Pueblo.

The trees around the pueblo were bare in keeping with their promise to keep Montezuma's fire burning. Ghosts floated above the demolished roofs, looking towards the sun, waiting for Montezuma.

She opened the pueblo gate and it creaked with rust.

A flickering light shone from a kiva and she climbed down the ladder. From the walls echoed Alfred V. Kidder's words from his May diary entry.

Old Jonesboro will turn green with envy. We have discovered ceremonial kivas of the pueblo religion still intact. The kivas are small rooms below the earth, reachable by ladder. We climbed down the ladder to enter a kiva from the entrance hole through which the sun's rays pitifully shone. The kiva lies between the underworld, which the Puebloans believed in, and the world above, so a bit like the Catholic purgatory, cool but confining. Wooden vigas support the wood ceiling and I must snap my hat off to the Indian genius in building such a spectacular cellar. There is even a fire pit. I am claustrophobic, a curse for an archaeologist. I began to hyperventilate as I wondered how it might have been when Indians and smoke filled the kiva, though there is that entrance hole, which acts as a ventilator and there is a deflector. It must have been elbowroom only then. The kiva has a hole in the floor, the Shipapu, which represents the place from which humans first emerged into daylight. The Indians believe spirits dwell there still. I expected one of these ghosts to rise from the hole and grab my ankle. I felt buried alive in this hellhole and yelled for Jack to come help me exit the kiva. My legs shook so bad when I climbed to the open air Jack helped me to my tent. I now know what an ant feels like.

Hollow-Woman saw no such spirits but could make out from the flicker of a dying fire, twelve virgins sleeping. The virgins were supposed to keep the fire continuously burning until Montezuma's return. She nudged one lazy virgin with her toe, but the girl would not awaken.

She ripped a piece of fabric from the woman's skirt and used this to protect her fingers as she grabbed a cinder from the fire of Montezuma's Altar of the Sun.

It seemed her theft had consequences. Montezuma's fire fizzled to ashes and left her in darkness, screaming, and struggling to find the ladder. She tripped over perhaps a virgin or two in her scramble to emerge from the blackness of the kiva and into the light.

The pueblo appeared even more haunting with no habitation. All the storage bins were empty of grain.

She opened the church door and an old man with white hair to his knees shocked her. Beside him, a goat chewed on a wooden floor.

"Welcome. You are just in time for lunch," he said.

He offered her a wooden bowl filled with blue corn meal, brimming with goat's milk.

She had no appetite but did not want to offend him so sat crosslegged on the floor and ate a few spoonfuls, keeping her eye on the decaying Catholic Church altar.

A hissing noise came from the old man and he flicked his long tongue at her. He transformed into a snake with feathers and swiveled towards the church door, slithering across the floor with a swishing noise.

She threw her bowl and ran after him.

The snake seemed to grow larger but moved so fast she couldn't catch it as it disappeared in a dust cloud the size of a tornado.

She ran through the gate to catch up with the others and tell them she found the Altar of the Sun and their feathered serpent. If they would come back and relight Montezuma's fire, all would prosper.

"See, I saved a piece in case we can't find the kiva again," she yelled and held up the cold cinder.

They paid no attention as they trudged up the trail with their shoulders slumped, dragging their feet.

Huffing and puffing, it was not much of a stretch to catch up with the starving Indians.

Along the way, she passed three who had succumbed to hunger. The others must not have had the strength to bury them.

She skidded to a stop where a man lay, gasping for breath.

My God, he looks just like Grandfather.

A younger man, who also bore a resemblance to Grandfather, held in his arms the dying old man whose ribs stuck out of his chest.

"Be strong, my son. Here is our ceremonial staff," he said, handing his son the silver staff which was not as tarnished as in present day. "You must guard it dearly, for you are now the keeper of the pride of the Pecos. If you do not survive, pass the staff to one of your cousins in this order: Dragon-Fly, Jose, Snow-Eagle-Down, Agustín, and Flint Society Rainbow," he said.

"I will, Father."

The old man gave a deep sigh and then his head fell back.

"Father," the younger man moaned, tearing at his shirt.

She could not stand to watch this man, probably her great-great-great-great-grandfather abandon his father's body. The dead man looked too much like Grandfather.

While the others straggled along the path to Jemez, she dug in the dirt with her hands then gave up because it was impossible to dig a grave this way. She unbuttoned her blouse and covered the old man with it.

She dropped the large cold cinder in her pocket and stumbled towards the direction of Pecos, clothed only in a camisole and jeans.

When she got to the pueblo gates, Grandfather barred her way.

"I am all business today," he said, running his hands down his black, double-breasted suit with pin-striped vest and red tie. He wore the diamond-studded cuff links that he wore the night they danced. "The pueblo is closed until the funeral decorations are ready."

"How many survived?" she said, her voice choking with tears.

"Only thirteen survived the journey to Jemez Pueblo. Seventeen collapsed and died, dotting the trail to Jemez with corpses," he said.

"Why did nobody care that they were starving? Pecos Village was close enough, filled with Spanish settlers who encroached on the lands of our people."

"Pecos became of no use to other pueblos, the plains Indians, the Spanish settlers, the governor of New Mexico, or the Catholic church. Such is the lot of the poor," he said.

"Jemez cared about Pecos."

"Because our brothers' language is also Towa so they could hear our cries. Isn't it tragic how lack of communication turns other human beings into castaways? Do you still have the burned out cinder from Montezuma's sacred fire or did you throw it away like trash?"

"Of course, I have the cinder. I would never throw magic away."

"Good. Perhaps one day, you will relight the fire at the Altar of the Sun. Here, this will fortify you so that you may finish your journey to bury your family."

She drank the brew he offered her.

With her last swallow, the dream catcher's wild spinning woke her in the hotel room and tears parched her throat.

Sunlight streamed through the window and on the pillow next to her, sparkled the cinder from Montezuma's fire, appearing like a black pearl on the white pillowcase, like Cinderella offered a jewel.

25

On May 19, a cloudy sixty degrees in Boston, a 53-foot semi-trailer filled with the bones of 2,067 men, women, and children, wound its way down Highway 90.

Each turn of the wheels distanced the Pecos bones from their foster home. The journey to the Pecos ruins would take about three days. She would bury her family and once more be the last of her kind above the earth.

I mustn't think of him as dead even though he rides in the trailer, bouncing on his mattress in a wooden coffin that Steve shipped from home. The coffin was made from pine trees of the Sangre de Cristo Mountains, as he requested the day she drove him to Pecos and he told her about the bones.

He united with his Pecos skeletons with centuries of chit-chat between them. She imagined him sitting in the trailer on one of the boxes, his face shining with a healthy glow, only one wrinkle on his face. He smoked his ceremonial pipe with his arm around a relative or new friend. He threw back his head and laughed at some joke. He slapped his buddy on the back and stomped his foot as joyous tears streamed down his cheeks.

She wanted to believe with all her heart that he at last found the peace that eluded him all his life. She had a new wrinkle on her face that showed up the day he died.

She sat next to the driver, a rough-looking man but very nice with ice-blue eyes. She didn't speak much during the trip. While the rig roared down the interstates, she closed her eyes and leaned her head back. The bones spoke to her and she answered. Every once in a while she would chant, singing some prayer in Towa.

"Please keep the radio off," she requested.

She communed with her ancestors as the rig's wheels spun faster towards New Mexico, sounding a lot like weaving machines of old, when the women made wool for winter blankets. The truck and rig sounded like sixteen weaving machines, one machine for each wheel, spinning a path towards home.

When they stopped in Las Vegas, New Mexico for lunch, they felt restlessness in the air.

"It's coming from the bones. The missing ones smell the scent of Pecos. It has been eighty-four years," she said to the driver.

Her chanting grew louder as the driver pointed his rig southwest on I-25 and they began the last forty-five miles to the upper Pecos Valley of New Mexico.

She instructed the driver to take the Rowe exit interchange 307.

The rig traveled north on New Mexico 63, the three miles to the Pecos Pueblo.

It seemed the trailer pulsed like hearts beating in a cardiac ward. At last, the bones were home.

She pointed out to him the Pecos ruins that rose from a rocky knoll in the center of a wide fertile valley near the Pecos River that flowed from the pine-covered Sangre de Cristo Mountains. "Part of the convento where the friars lived still stands," she said, jabbing her finger towards a bit of wall. "The friars' workshops, tanneries, stables, corrals, kitchen, gardens and dining room melted back into the earth from where they came. I've seen this place in my dreams, as it once was, the land of a glorious civilization. Pecos Pueblo was wonderful to look at in those days. My people's ways were so different; the Spanish rammed their own values and way of life down their throats. By the time the Comanches made peace with Pecos in 1786, hundreds had died at their hands over nearly a century of harassment. Trade resumed with Pecos for a dozen years and it looked like we were on our way to recovery but then the Comancheros came."

"What are Comancheros?" he said, picking at his teeth with a toothpick.

"The Spanish who did not trade at fairs but transported their goods directly to the Comanches, who had by then replaced the Apaches, through brute force, as the main exporters and importers. Comancheros also traded directly with the pueblos and became the middlemen between the plains Indians, the Spanish, and the pueblos. It meant the beginning of the end for my people until they had no choice but to leave or starve. No one has lived here for the past 161 years, and much of the adobe melted back into the soil from whence it came until all that remains is a ghost pueblo. It's almost a dream now, as if Pecos never was. The proof of its existence though is the bones in your trailer."

He ground his rig to a halt, the brakes squeaking and red dust blowing around the tires.

The day of the dead arrived and life rebounded full circle.

26

Steve was a Jemez man and dressed in a red, colorful Southwestern shirt, cowboy hat and boots. Splashes of turquoise decorated his belt buckle. A watch, attached to a silver band dotted with turquoise, hugged his wrist. A magnificent turquoise and silver squash necklace hung around his neck.

She planned to bury the bones together in one large grave. Steve and his friends had dug the grave, not disturbing any tree roots or other Pecos remains, by using information NASA transmitted from radar that penetrated the ground

One by one, Steve's friends gently lifted the bones from their boxes and placed them within the grave.

It was a dry spring, the ground so hard it seemed the ruins conspired with the elements to freeze the earth so that the bones would never be disturbed again.

She dressed like the ancients with a colorful, striped, wool blanket tied at her shoulder and a red and black palm-width sash tied at her waist. Over her shoulders was draped a cape made from white turkey feathers.

A rumbling in the earth came from the west. Wave after wave of Native Americans, dressed in their colorful finest, dotted the Pecos hills, making the pueblo appear to come to life.

"Two hundred walked from Jemez to Pecos to commemorate the journey made by the thirteen survivors. They have walked the same trail of tears and cried along the way," Steve said.

"They remembered; the Pecos people have not been forgotten."

"Because of you, Sweetheart, all due to you," he said, taking her in his arms and holding her quivering body.

"No, because of Grandfather," she said, wiping her damp cheeks.

She walked alone in front of the mourners who sprinkled cornmeal along the burial walk to the single massive grave.

Steve, Jerry Norberto's nephew, and four other nephews of Grandfather's friends carried a wooden pueblo ladder upon which his corpse lay.

She walked beside them and with each step, sprinkled corn meal on his body.

She pounded the ceremonial staff against the ground. I am of the snake clan of Pecos. With each pounding of the staff, her heart beat with the pride of a ghost nation.

The mourners traversed the grave, counterclockwise, until they walked full circle.

The men placed him in the center of the grave, squatting on his blanket, facing east like a rising sun.

She would remember him in death this way: top-half of his face painted sun-yellow above a bottom-half blue sky; feather rays of sunlight encircling his head to light the darkness in the grave; him holding court at the center of 2,067 skeletons fanning out around him; his precious bones to keep him company through all eternity. His arms were decorated with feather rays, spread like the wings of an eagle to cast the sun's warmth upon the bones.

Wind blew her cape around her shoulders and she opened her own wings to the heavens and sang out her thanks in Towa. She sang the story of the golden age of Pecos, how a once proud people founded a pueblo in 1300 and eventually grew to be two thousand. The men were such strong warriors and the pueblo so formidable.

She thanked the sun, the clouds, the rain, all the animals and the Kachinas for bringing home the missing. She dropped to her knees and held her hands over the bones, like she was blessing them. She told them what happened to cause their displacement and confusion. She explained to the bones the reason they were gone from home for so long and where they went.

"Please forgive the archaeologist because he did not understand his sacrilege of disturbing your rest and taking you so far from your homeland. It took an act of Congress to allow you to come home, and your country did not let the people down this time. You will never be disturbed again. The sustenance of this earth will strengthen you and the rays of Grandfather, Sun Kachina, will light your way. I wish you all joy on your crossing. I pray you have a gentle ride to the other side. I look forward to one day joining my ancestors."

The hollow sockets of the skulls stared up at her, and the ground shook beneath the kivas.

Steve stepped forward and spoke to the mourners. "On November 13, 1901 in the hour before dusk folds to night, a mist swirled the summit of Chicoma Mountain, creating a cloud shaped like an Indian tipi. A moon bloated with light tap-danced across the sky and slid into the tipi cloud the exact moment Great-Grandmother cruised into labor. For a few hours, the moon peeked through the flap of the tipi cloud, as if awaiting a stupendous birth. As soon as Grandfather was born, the cloud slowly evaporated, appearing as if smoke blew from the tipi on the mountain top. With each smoke exhalation by the moon, a scent of herbs and tobacco engulfed Jemez Pueblo. The elders predicted that this child, born under a never-before-seen tipi moon, was a channel to the spirit world. The elders' prophecy came true; Grandfather became a master of magic."

"He was leader of the snake clan so he shed his skin and adapted in an ever-changing world. He faced life with the daring of a hawk and the humor of a raccoon. As Clown Society member, he drained laughter from gloomy depths of souls. The power of a mountain lion pulsed through his veins. As medicine chief, he rescued spellbound hearts from witches. He mastered the abracadabra of sorcery with the slyness of a fox. As Kachina priest, he ruled the supernatural world. When decked out for ceremony with feather rays, he embodied the spirit of Sun Kachina. As Kachina priest with gift of thunderstorms, he seduced crops with liquid sunshine. He was special friend to Coyote Kachina, who taught him the secret of shape shifting."

"Grandfather blessed this earth with his presence for ninety-eight years. He had the courage to survive and left this world a better place than he found it. We shall all miss him."

She blew a kiss at Grandfather. "Goodbye, Governor. You are my sun beneath the earth, my heart above the clouds, and my prayer for a better life. I will see you every morning when the sun rises. I shall miss you when the sun sets. I will yearn for you on a cloudy day. Do not forget me." She threw a silver locket with her picture into the grave.

The men shoveled dirt on the burial site.

In the center on top were Grandfather's favorite dish of beans and chile, and a bottle of water, waiting for him so he would not hunger or thirst on his journey. His spirit would haunt the Pecos ruins four days before transforming into a Kachina. He would then travel to Kachina Village. He had his Kachina mask with him and he would wear it at the banquet set for him. His spiritual protector, Sun Kachina would welcome him.

There. It was done. The men set down their shovels.

Mists of clouds began to gather.

She cocked her ear to the wind.

"Listen to my ancestors continuing their journey, interrupted when their bones were exhumed. I have been cursed, but now the curse is lifted. I returned my family to their land so they can rest peacefully. Now, the Pecos will flourish once more. We will have children and multiply," she said.

"I'm sure we will, Holly," Steve said.

He stood behind her and placed his hands on her waist.

She lifted her head to the sky.

"Do you see them?" she said.

"All I see is a sky filled with billowy white clouds."

"The spirits of my ancestors are now at rest and have become Cloud People. They crossed the bridge and Pautiwa, Chief of Kachina Village welcomes them."

"The sky looked clear before we buried the bones, and now I've never seen so many clouds before, must be thousands. You remind me of Grandfather," he said, hugging her in his arms like he might never let her go.

"Do you mind if I stay a little while by myself?" she said.

He left her sitting by the burial ground still staring up at the sky.

The bones weren't the only ones who had come home. She smiled up at a cloud that bore Grandfather's features.

The cloud dissipated, and at last, he traveled on his way.

Other clouds, the spirits of the bones, followed him across the heavens.

As they passed, she saw her own features in the clouds, generations of grandparents, cousins, aunts, and uncles.

Grandfather once told her: when you learn to love unselfishly, when you learn to not want so much, then you will no longer be Hollow-Woman.

Through shimmering tears, she blinked at the fluffy clouds and felt fullness within and knew she would never be hollow again.

She walked over to her mother's grave and imagined below this earth, sitting alone in a corner, a skeleton wore a necklace. Her chin bone touched the tip of her chest bone. Her hip bones were spread, as if she had just given birth.

"Mama," she cried, falling to her knees.

The heart-shaped necklace lit up and a heartbeat fluttered in her mother's ribcage.

She swore she felt her mother's hand bones squeeze her hands.

Her mother's eye sockets stared at her in a droopy-dog way.

Her big teeth grinned at her.

She heard her mother's voice: My spirit calls to you in never-ending song like two birds seeking each other in darkness. Forever, I am drawn to my baby. You are my light. I am so very proud of you.

She stroked her mother's grave and sang back to her.

"From your lips sings the music of angels. I feel you in my heart and in the depths of my very soul. I have been so lost without you," she said, touching her forehead to the sacred dirt.

For one moment in time, one precious moment, the gate to the other world crept open and a beautiful young Indian maiden with black shimmering hair brushing her shoulders, stood before her with her hands reaching out to her.

Before she could touch her, the woman was lifted up to the sky and her mother's face formed in a cloud, hovered above her a minute, then floated across the sky to join the others.

27

Her dream catcher swirled clockwise around her head, and she waited at the foot of the Sangre de Cristo Mountains.

Ah. Here they come.

Some thirty weary souls walked towards Pecos.

She wished she had brought some food and water with her.

The closer they got, the stronger they seemed to grow until all thirty stood tall. Their flesh glowed with life. The eldest wore a silver crown with turquoise beads. She should know this man, yet his name escaped her.

"You have always known me for I have never left you," he said, smiling gently at her. "We've come to give you this."

He handed her a slab of wood newly cut from a tree of the Sangre de Cristo Mountains. A polished image of the lady was carved in the center of the slab.

"Thank you. I'll always cherish this gift," she said.

"Have faith," he said, bowing his head to her.

He turned, and walked towards the Pecos ruins. He pounded against the earth the royal staff given to the people by King Phillip III of Spain. The man walked like he was somebody.

The others followed.

She tried to yell at them not to leave her, but couldn't squeeze the words from her dry throat.

She wanted to run after them but her feet would not move.

A finger tapped her shoulder.

She held her breath and turned slowly.

It was him.

"You have done well, Child," he said, stroking her cheek with a gnarled hand.

"You act surprised that I succeeded in the task you gave me."

"Granddaughter, you have always misunderstood. You are my joy and my shining pride. I believe in your strength, for the Pecos River runs through your blood. Your heart beats within this earth. At last, you have become the woman I always knew you could be."

She clung to his sleeve but he spun on his white moccasins and ran as fast as a deer to catch the other Pecos spirits.

"Don't cry," a soft voice said.

Through her tears she saw her mother pull the sleeve of a man who seemed hesitant to approach her. He grabbed her mother's hand and pulled her to join the others who waited for them. Warriors, women and children, vanished from the horizon.

The sun seemed to melt the thirty-three souls back into the earth and the dirt shimmered like yellow glass.

Behind her echoed the laughter of ghost children.

Above the black and white stripes of her bed, her dream catcher spun clockwise in the direction of good dreams, slowing, until it stopped.

She hugged the wooden slab of the Lady that once hung from the church walls. She held up the slab in wonder. The wood appeared newly cut from a pine tree of the Sangre de Cristo Mountains. The lady sparkled as if varnished.

This was his gift to her, not just a dream catcher to decorate her ceiling, but faith and belief in family.

EPILOGUE

With a heavy heart, she drove to Pecos.

She sat in her SUV for ten minutes, clenching the wheel with white knuckles.

She squinted to see the ghost buildings of five-story apartments. All she saw was the ruins.

She cocked her ear for the laughter of children, the gossip of women and the labor of men. All she heard was the flutter of a breeze.

She rolled down the windows and sniffed for baking bread but all she smelled was dirt.

She peered at the church ruins for Franciscans clothed in monks' robes, rosary beads clanking against their knees, hoods bowed and chanting novenas. All she saw were graves of the friars she brought back from Boston, buried where she estimated their beds had been. The convento at Pecos had been their home and they, too, deserved the peace of reburial.

She let out a deep sigh, unbuckled her seat belt and got down.

David, her nine-year-old, pounded the ceremonial staff against the ground as he walked beside her. He was governor of the Pecos ruins, an honor he did not take lightly. He was so like Grandfather and Steve already indoctrinated him into Kachina society.

"What's wrong, Mama? You seem so sad," David said.

"Yeah, every time you bring us to Pecos, you cry," said Maria, who was eight. She was wise like Grandfather and a straight-A student.

Maria held the hand of Sammy, her youngest and six years-old. Sammy was a good candidate for Clown Society.

"I'm just crying from happiness because I have you kids. Our family ruins are a magical place," she said.

"Because of Great-Grandfather," Sammy said.

She led her children to the mass grave.

"Great-Grandfather is buried here and brings the sun to us," David said.

"He visits us in his sweat lodge," Maria said.

"What?!" Holly said. "Oh, but he comes as a cloud."

"No, he doesn't," David said.

"Great-Grandfather says love never dies," Sammy said.

"That's right, children, love never dies," she said through her tears, "nor does faith, nor hope, nor magic."

For the umpteenth time she sang to her children in Towa, the story of Pecos, their once mighty pueblo that ruled this land.

When she finished the tale of their ancestors, David, Maria, and Sammy recited: "And when Montezuma returns, Pecos will ascend from the earth like a Phoenix rising from the ashes."

She pulled from her purse the cinder from the sacred fire of Montezuma and with a match, lit a flame with the ember.

As governor of Pecos Pueblo, David took the burning ember.

All four faced east, like their ancestors had for centuries, their eyes scanning the morning star, waiting for Montezuma to return to his Altar of the Sun.

The wind picked up and the ember glowed red.

Holly laughed at dust swirling like brown ghosts around her ankles.

And she heard the wind whisper in Towa: you have done well, child.

Grandfather's face smiled down at them from a cloud.

And at the ruins, the pueblo came to life and the Pecos ghosts danced.

AN AFTERWORD BY THE AUTHOR

For my novel, *The Witch Narratives Reincarnation*, I was researching the Native American legend about Montezuma once ruling Pecos Pueblo, when I came across an article in the Harvard Gazette about the repatriation of the Pecos Bones. These skeletons became very real for me, and I felt heartbroken by the fact that they had been taken from their resting place and "put to work" at Harvard, i.e. enslaved, for 85 years.

Their reburial back at the ghost pueblo of Pecos really moved me, and I felt as if these bones were reaching out to me, asking me to tell their story. The more I researched, the more passionate I became about the Pecos skeletons.

I visited the ruins of the Pecos Pueblo but could not visit the secret burial site. Nevertheless, I promised the bones that though the Pecos people are extinct, the world should not forget the skeletons that contributed so much to mankind.

I came up with the title *Return of the Bones* and created the fictional last of the Pecos people, Hollow-Woman and Grandfather, who venture to claim their family and bring the bones home for reburial.

The result is this book, told with much heart and many tears shed while writing it.

INTERACTIVE LINKS

VIDEOS
Some ghosts of Pecos dancing
The Skull & Bones letter news video
The Ghost Pueblo of Pecos happy to be reunited with the missing bones
Cloud People of Pecos
In Memoriam
Ishi, the Last Yahi
Sand Creek Massacre

OTHER
America's oldest Madonna 1625
Ceremonial kivas
Colonel John Chivington wanted to exterminate the Indian, but was anti-slavery
Coyote
Don Juan de Oñate
Dr. Alfred V. Kidder wiki
Dr. Alfred V. Kidder and the Pecos archaeological dig
Dream Catcher
Fort Lyon Arapahoe Peace Treaty
Franciscan Friars
Francisco Vasquez de Coronado & the Spanish Conquistadors
Francisco Vasquez de Coronado wiki
Fray Bernal, Agent of the Spanish Inquisition
Franz Boas, Anthropologist wiki
Indian Pueblo Revolt in 1680 in New Mexico(with audio)
Ishi, the last surviving Yahi
Katsinam
Kokopelli
Masawkatsina

Men disguised as Kachinas
Minik
Mudhead
NAGPRA
Native American Tears
North complex of Pecos Pueblo around 1450
Our Lady of Light, Patrona of the Pecos people
Palace of the Governors
Pautiwa
Pecos Mission
Popé (Po-pay) statue in Washington DC
Return of the Bones website
Robert Peary, modern explorer wiki
Ruins of Pecos Pueblo
Sand Creek Massacre wiki
Seven Cities of Gold
Shipapu
Spanish Inquisition
Squash-blossom
Squash necklace
Study Guide
The End of the Trail sculptor
The End of the Trail Statue
The Witch Narratives: Reincarnation
Trail of Tears wiki
Yowi

About the Author

Belinda Vasquez Garcia is an award-winning, best-selling, critically acclaimed author. Before writing full time, she worked as a Software Engineer and Web Developer. She holds a Bachelor's degree in Applied Mathematics from the University of New Mexico. She is a native of California. She lives with her husband Bob, dog Toby, and cat Shakespeare.

She is the author of THE BIGAMIST, A Memoir of My Father, and THE WOMANIZER, Another Memoir of My Father.

Her first book in the Land of Enchantment Trilogy, The Witch Narratives Reincarnation, is a first place winner of the 2013 Latino Books into Movies Awards. The book was, also, a 2013 Best Fantasy International Latino Book Awards Winner, and a 2012 Best Fantasy New Mexico / Arizona Book Awards Finalist. The story continues in Ghosts of the Black Rose (Land Of Enchantment Trilogy Book 2), a 2013 Best Fantasy New Mexico / Arizona Book Awards Finalist.

Lastly, she would like to thank you for purchasing Return of the Bones.

LINKS:

http://www.facebook.com/AuthorBelinda(Fan page)

http://www.twitter.com/MagicPros (Twitter - Belinda V. Garcia@ MagicProse)

http://belindavasquezgarcia.com/blog/ (Blog)

http://belindavasquezgarcia.com (website).

Her YouTube channel is Belinda V Garcia.

GLOSSARY

alabado
Spanish word for a morbid hymn sung at funerals and wakes.

brujo
Spanish word for a male witch.

Capítan
Spanish word for Captain.

Cicuye
The original name for the Pecos Pueblo until the Spanish explorer Don Juan de Oñate renamed it Pecos.

convento
Spanish word for convent or monastery.

Cloud People
In pueblo society, the dead can inhabit clouds or make clouds with their breath. The clouds are considered ancestors who bring rain.

Clown Society
A Pueblo ceremonial organization that provides comic relief and also, instills fear.

Coyote
A Kachina known as the Trickster.

Don Juan de Oñate
First colonial governor of New Mexico. He ruled from 1598 to 1608.

Forked Lightning People
Archaeologists discovered the Forked Lightning Ruin half a mile below the Pecos Pueblo, which was estimated to have been occupied between 1225 and 1300 and housed hundreds of Native Americans. These groups combined to build the Pecos pueblo.

Francisco Vasquez de Coronado
The Spanish explorer did not initially go to Pecos in 1540 but sent an expedition of around twenty, led by Captain Hernando de Alvarado. Around 1541, Coronado with around 1500 knights, Tiwa slaves and Indian allies, traveled to Pecos to ask for their help.

Custos
The head of the Franciscan friars in New Mexico, sort of like what an Archbishop is to priests.

Encomendero
A Spaniard given an income from a pueblo or pueblos, paid as a tribute of taxes. The income was given for three successive lifetimes so was inherited. The tributes were normally given as crops, animal hides, blankets and whatever economy a pueblo could provide.

encomíenda
A pueblo providing an income for a Spaniard.

encomíenda tax
A tribute required to be paid by a pueblo to the Spaniard to whom it is given.

flageolet
A flute-like instrument made from the bones of a bird.

Franciscans
A Catholic religious order.

Fray
A Spanish word meaning brother.

Geronimo
An Apache leader and medicine man from New Mexico.

harquebus (also spelled arquebus)
A rifle-like weapon used in the 15th to 17th centuries and in-vented by Spain. The first weapon fired at the shoulder. If fired at close range, a harquebus could pierce armor. It was loaded at the muzzle with a range less than 650 feet.

Healing Society
A Pueblo ceremonial organization providing healing.

Hispaño
Spanish word for Spaniard.

horno oven
An outdoor wood-burning oven made of adobe, shaped like a beehive.

Kachina
A powerful spirit-being who lives half the year at the pueblo to benefit the community as rainmakers and provide growth for humankind. During religious ceremonies, masked dancers em-body Kachinas, wearing masks that depict the Kachina they are impersonating.

Kachina Priest
A pueblo man who oversees prayer meetings. He blesses the pueblo and calls up the divine Kachinas.

Kachina Village
The home of the dead for members of Kachina society, which includes the majority of Pueblo men.

Katsina
A Kachina is a powerful Native American spirit being originally called a Katsina in ancient days.

Katsinam
More than one Katsina; i.e. plural form of the word Katsina.

kiva
A circular ceremonial room located underground like a basement. A ladder is used to enter and exit the kiva through a hole on top.

Kokopelli
Fertility god.

Madonna
The mother of Jesus.

maize
Also known as corn. Introduced by the American Indian and given to the white man as a gift. The staple domestic food crop of the pueblos.

mal ojo
Spanish for evil eye. A person with this power can curse people just by staring at them.

Masawkatsina
A Kachina who is keeper of the dead and rules the underworld. He is the only Kachina to live in the fourth world, which is the present world so he exists as an earth god. One myth has it that the third world was destroyed by a flood but the Puebloans used hollow reeds as boats and emerged into the fourth world at the Shipapu of the kiva.

middle path
Though some Puebloans converted to Catholicism most separated Catholic beliefs and Pueblo beliefs and tried to live both ways.

Moctezuma
The name given Montezuma by the Puebloans.

Montezuma
The famous Aztec ruler. Pueblo legend claims that he was a great witch born in the ancient Pose Uingge Pueblo in New Mexico and founded the pueblos that exist today. He then turned into an eagle and flew south to Mexico to build Mexico City.

Mudhead
A clown-like Kachina made of mud that carries the footprints of humans on its head. His birth is the result of an incestuous relationship between brother and sister.

NAGPRA
Stands for Native American Graves and Protection Repatriation Act and was passed into federal law on November 16, 1990. The law requires agencies that receive funds from the U.S. government to return the remains of Native Americans and cultural items to respective tribes. Federal grants provide financial assistance in the repatriation.

Nunna daul Tsuny
Comanche for *Trail of Tears*.

Nuevo México
Spanish for New Mexico. New Spain included Mexico and New Mexico which was formally named by Oñate though it was first called Nuevo México by Francisco de Ibarra, who traveled north from Mexico seeking gold mines in 1563.

papoose
A Native American infant.

Pautiwa
A sun Kachina and chief of the other Kachina spirits.

Patrona
A Spanish word meaning patroness.

Pose Uingge
An ancient, New Mexico pueblo purported to be the birthplace of Montezuma. The pueblo was excavated twenty miles north of San Juan Pueblo. Discovered among the ruins are skeletons with their skulls crushed.

Río Grande
Spanish for Grand River. The river snakes from lower Colorado through central New Mexico and along the western line of Texas. The Rio Grande is the Texas border between Mexico and the U.S.

Quetzalcoatl
A Mesoamerican feathered serpent deity worshipped by Aztecs, Toltecs, Mayans, and other groups.

Quivira and the Seven Cities of Gold
The Spanish explorer, Francisco Vasquez de Coronado, came to the New World searching for the fabled Seven Cities of Gold. In 1541, he claimed to have found a place called Quivira where golden cups supposedly hung from trees. Gold did not exist at Coronado's Quivira, only a few tipis. However, the Spanish continued to search for Quivira as late as 1678.

Sangre de Cristo
A Spanish phrase meaning "blood of Christ".

Santa Fe
The capital of New Mexico and the oldest capital city in the United States, founded in 1608. Santa Fe was originally occupied by Indian villages in 1050.

Santos
A Spanish word meaning saints.

Shipapu
The doorway to the gods; the place where human souls are kept and emerge from; the place where man first emerged. Located at every pueblo, the entrance to Shipapu is a hole in a kiva.

Skull and Bone's Society
A secret society at Yale University whose members encompass elite, wealthy students and alumni.

Spanish Inquisition
A Catholic tribunal used to accuse heretics, imprison them, execute them, and seize their property for the church.

Sun Kachina
A spirit of the sun god.

tamale
An Indian and Mexican dish which originated with the Aztecs. A paste is made from corn meal and spread on a corn husk. Meat filling is placed in the paste and the tamale is then folded and steamed.

Tiwa
The pueblo language spoken by Isleta, Sandia, Picuris and Taos Pueblos.

Tiwas
The group of Puebloans who speak Tiwa as their native language.

Towa
The language spoken by Jemez and Pecos pueblos.

vigas
A type of Southwest style ceiling beam, often decorative.

Yowi
An ogre Kachina who beheaded priests during the Indian Pueblo Revolt in 1680 in New Mexico.

Zunis
Members of the Zuni Pueblo.

B-I-B-L-I-O-G-R-A-P-H-Y

Benedict, Ruth, Patterns of Culture, Mariner Books, January 25, 2006.

Block, Ira. "At Rest, at Last!" National Geographic Magazine, May, 1999.

Branch, Mark Alden; Lassila, Kathrin Day. "Whose Skull and Bones?" Yale Alumni Magazine, May/June 2006.

Brown, Dee. Bury My Heart At Wounded Knee: An Indian History of the American West, Henry Holt and Co., Anv edition, January 23, 2001.

Bullis, Don. New Mexico & Politicians of the Past, Rio Grande Books, November 10, 2008.

Bullock, Alice. Living Legends of the Santa Fe Country: A Collection of Southwestern Stories, Sunstone Press, November 30, 1990.

Fine-Dare, Kathleen Sue. Grave Injustice: the American Indian Repatriation Movement and NAGPRA (Fourth World Rising), University of Nebraska Press, October 1, 2002.

Gewertz, Ken. "The Long Voyage Home: Peabody returns Native American Remains to Pecos Pueblo" The Harvard University Gazette, May 20, 1999.

Goodheart, Adam. "Going Home" Harvard Magazine, September-October, 1998.

Gilbert, Joan. The Trail of Tears across Missouri (Missouri Heritage Readers Series), University of Missouri Press, June 1996.

Harper, Kenn. Give Me My Father's Body: The Life of Minik, the New York Eskimo, Washington Square Press, February 27, 2001.

Hoig, Stan. The Sand Creek Massacre, University of Oklahoma Press, 1974.

Kessell, John L. Kiva, Cross and Crown—The Pecos Indians and New Mexico, 1540-1840, Southwest Parks & Monuments Association, 2 edition, January 31, 1995.

O'Brien, Dennis. "Returning Bones Is a Daunting Task" Baltimore Sun, Jan. 12, 2004.

Prince, L. Bradford. Spanish Mission Churches of New Mexico, Nabu Press, Feb 16, 2010.

Robbins, Catherine C. "Pueblo Indians Receive Remains of Ancestors" The New York Times, May 23, 1999.

Simmons, Marc. Witchcraft in the Southwest—Spanish & Indian Supernaturalism on the Rio Grande, University of Nebraska Press, March 1, 1980.

Slayman, Andrew L. Archaeology: A publication of the Archaeological Institute of America, Volume 52 Number 4, July/August 1999.

Tarpy, Cliff. "Pueblo Ancestors Return Home" National Geographic Magazine, May, 1999.

Walter, Mariko Namba; Fridman, Eva Jane Neumann. Shamanism: An Encyclopedia of World Beliefs, Practices, and Culture, Volume 1, ABC-CLIO, December 15, 2004.

Wilson, James. The Earth Shall Weep: A History of Native America, Grove Press; 1st Grove Press Ed edition, March 3, 2000.

Made in the USA
Lexington, KY
06 May 2016